Abundance
for Life, Love
and Money

Linda Gabriel reveals the power of the mind & the Spirit within. She shows you how to change your life, by changing your mind.

Kevin G. Flicker
www.TheProsperityReview.com

Abundance for Life, Love and Money will give you the tools you need to create a life you love, no matter what your age!

Mary Ann Halpin
photographer and author of
Fearless Women: Midlife Portraits

Linda is an accomplished workshop leader and a great healer. Her work is ever evolving, influenced by her fresh experiences in her own journey and dedication to Spirit.

Gabrielle Beard
Founder www.TriWisdom.com
and www.womenandwisdom.org

Abundance
for Life, Love
and Money

by Linda Gabriel with Luke Chao

BURMANBOOKS
.com

Published by BurmanBooks Inc.
4 Lamay Cres. Scarborough, Ontario Canada M1X 1J1

BURMANBOOKS
.com

Gabriel, Linda
The Inner Power Series for Abundance for Life, Love and Money /
Linda Gabriel

Cover Design by www.AliveDesign.com

Edited by Solidus Communications www.solidus.ca

Typesetting by TypeWorx

Distribution:

Canada: Jaguar Book Group,
100 Armstrong Avenue
Georgetown, Ontario L7G 5S4

United States: Independent Publishers Group,
814 North Franklin Street,
Chicago, Ill 60610

ISBN 0-9736632-7-8

Other Burman Books Available:

The Inner Power Series:

For Golfers and Other Athletes
Seducing Your Man
Intuitive Security for Women
Abundance for Life, Love and Money
Anxiety and Depression

Call Waiting (fiction)

You are always welcome to visit
www.BurmanBooks.com

.

For my sons, William and Charlie.

Acknowledgements

I am deeply indebted to my many teachers, both physical and non-physical.

Thanks to my mom and sisters. Mom, you are such an inspiration as a woman, a colleague and a friend.

Thanks, Kristen for always being there.

A special thanks to Mary for letting me borrow your laptop keyboard even though you also were on a writing deadline.

I am grateful for the co-stars of my life Larry, Charlie, William and Chris.

Thanks to Luke Chao for helping me get my words on paper and to Catherine Jenkins for being a dream of an editor. Thanks to Sanjay Burman for his confidence in me and for his vision and audacity.

Thanks to Julie Benkofsky Webb who first asked me to teach. And finally, thank you to all my students, clients and friends who encourage me to write.

Table of Contents

Publisher's Foreword

I've been working in the film industry since I was fourteen years old. My achievements include producing a national show by the time I was seventeen, becoming a vice president of my own division in the country's largest talent agency and producing a movie that won awards all over the world by the time I was twenty-five.

However, I *still* wasn't achieving financial rewards or a less difficult struggle. The more I tried, the more I was stopped by hurdles placed in my way. I even had contracts from Showtime Cable FedExed to me, and the deal die while they were on their way to me!

Was I unlucky? Was I destined to be poor and struggling forever? Heck, I've achieved more than some people do in a lifetime! How, and why, was I in this position?

One day, while reading a letter one of my own clients had written, libeling me to many industry insiders, I thought my life was finally over. I'd be just one more person who couldn't make it in Hollywood and had to leave.

During my tantrum, I threw a magazine on the ground and saw an ad for hypnosis lessons. The teacher and I met, and she invited me to take her class. It turned my life around. I came to understand the power of hypnosis and realize the amazing changes it could enable.

While under hypnosis, I was asked what I'd do with a million dollars. My answer? Pay my debt, which totaled $50,000. My teacher acknowledged that, then waited for the rest of my list. There was nothing to add. In all honesty, I had no other reason for making so much money.

My teacher leaned closer to my ear and whispered, "When you find out what you actually need money for, you will have it."

I'd been trained in the "Hollywood way," to be greedy and destructive to myself and others. Through hypnosis I had discovered my true gift was to heal, and accordingly, a healer only uses what he needs. I visualized myself with lots of green bags filled with money. So many, I was overflowing with bags! She asked me, "What are you doing with them?"

"Giving them away," I replied. "There are too many for me, so I'm giving them away."

The next day, I started a company, the company that published this book. Because I wanted to share the secrets that are hidden within you, I was given the money immediately. People were writing too many checks! The two books I initially wanted to publish turned into seven in the first season alone.

I feel great relief that now, money is there when I need it. I trust myself and my intuition, so now I don't fret over deals, I don't wait by the phone for people to get back to me and I surely don't worry "will it happen?" Everything in life now "happens if it's supposed to." And it does!

Sanjay Burman

Chapter 1:
An Epiphany*

The fellow on TV held a 100,000-year-old human skull in his hands. It was late at night and I couldn't sleep. I was channel surfing, but there wasn't much on, so I paused to listen to the man with the skull. It was a program about the history of the human species and he was speaking about modern humans, *Homo sapiens sapiens,* or "thinking man." He was saying that current research indicates that *Homo sapiens sapiens* have been on Earth for as long as 90,000 to 130,000 years. Then casually, just as an aside, he commented that if we were to clone a child from the DNA of that 100,000-year-old human skull and raise him in a modern family, the child would be indistinguishable from a modern child.

In that instant, I had an epiphany. I realized that evolution was not what I had believed. Human evolution wasn't about growing a different kind of thumb or toe or developing a better, more adaptable body. It wasn't even about developing a bigger and better brain. All the action in human evolution for over 100,000 years has been in the realm of consciousness: how we think about things.

---

* Epiphany: a usually sudden manifestation or perception of the essential nature or meaning of something; an intuitive grasp of reality through something (as an event) usually simple and striking; an illuminating discovery; a revealing scene or moment.

Everything Begins with a Thought

One hundred thousand years ago, the world was quite different. People lived as hunter-gatherers. We didn't have cars, computers or skyscrapers. There were no books, music or medications. All the raw materials humans have used to create, have existed in the world all along. Yet the human mind cannot create what it has not first imagined.

Everything ever made by humans—every car, building, movie, every book, basket or loaf of bread—began with a thought. Sometimes it can seem that a computer, or a building or a Shakespearean sonnet simply gave rise to itself, but it's actually a product of human imagination. Nothing in the physical world has been added or taken away, only changed. That shows the power of thought. Thoughts create things.

Science now knows that thoughts create biological events. Neurotransmitters are present everywhere in the body, not just in the brain. The new science of psychoneuroimmunology describes how a thought precipitates a cascade of biochemical events in the body. These events dramatically influence the health and well-being of an individual throughout life. Candace Pert, M.D. describes them as "molecules of emotion" and has written a book with that title. Thought creates emotion and our emotions influence how we each experience our reality.

If we understand that thought is the source of our emotions, we might want to pay attention to what we're thinking. Indeed, Candace Pert says that the medicine of the future will start with three basic questions: 1) What do you eat? 2) How do you move? and 3) *What are your thoughts?* Unfortunately, most of the time, most of us don't have a clue what we are actually thinking.

As a man thinketh, so he is.

—Proverbs 23:7

The Little Voice

Have you ever noticed "The Little Voice" inside your mind? I don't mean the voice of Intuition, although The Little Voice might like you to believe that's what it is. I mean The Little Voice that sounds like a TV voice-over providing a running commentary of opinions, facts, beliefs and judgments about your experiences, other people and especially about yourself. It judges what's good or bad, acceptable or unacceptable, believable or ridiculous. The Little Voice often functions as a filter for what you are willing to accept and especially what you are going to reject.

While it's useful to know what you like and don't like— Chocolate? *Yes!* Licorice? *No!*—for many people, The Little Voice tends to be a powerful inner critic that can obstruct their ability to experience joy and success in life. The Little Voice keeps a significant part of your attention focused in the past or future, distracted from the present moment. The problem is that these thoughts are habitual. They're often irrational and certainly unexamined, automatic responses created by your subconscious mind. These automatic patterns of thought become filters through which you perceive reality—filters which may not be the most beneficial for you. However, you don't experience your filters as filters you experience them as *reality!* Even more insidious, you may experience your filters as *the real you*. Let me assure you, you are not your filters!

Buddhists call this inner voice "monkey mind," because it's always chattering and busy. Meditation is an ancient practice that helps quiet The Little Voice. In that silence, you have an opportunity to experience your identity as separate from your Little Voice. Some call that moment of realization Enlightenment.

One of the things The Little Voice provides is a sense of security. If reality changes too dramatically, The Little Voice is likely to sound a danger signal. It will say no and step on the brakes. It's easy to feel a sense of security within the familiar territory of the status quo. The Little Voice would rather not change it's opinions, thank you very much. What the Little Voice loves most of all is to be *right!* Right is safe. Right is secure.

This is why it seems some people would rather be right, than be rich, happy or free. It would be more accurate to say The Little Voice would rather be right than *allow* them to be rich, happy or free. When threatened, The Little Voice is not above recruiting a few anxiety attacks, because it knows that fear freezes flow. It will call on fears that are subconscious, so the person doesn't even know why they feel afraid to move forward in their lives, even though consciously, they very much desire to.

I encourage you not to let The Little Voice stop you from trying new ideas. Remember The Little Voice is conditioned, automatic thinking that may not have been tested since you were two or three years old. The Little Voice is very skilled at pretending it's the voice of knowledge or wisdom, when it's really just another opinion. Begin to notice what The Little Voice says; invite it to tea, in a way. Find out how it works and what it's thinking. You may be very surprised.

Once you have tuned into The Little Voice, you can decide whether or not what it says is helpful in any given situation. If it is, great! If not, just say "Thanks for sharing," and do what the real you knows is best.

But there's an even better way to deal with The Little Voice. It can be retrained through hypnotherapy, guided visualization and affirmations. Affirmations are positive statements you repeat to yourself over and over. One of the ways the subconscious mind learns is through repetition. Perhaps The Little Voice is thinking, "Money doesn't grow on trees, you know!" You can teach it a new habit, to think a different automatic thought, one that's much more empowering like, "Money is created by human energy and human imagination. I create my own wealth easily and effortlessly."

Chapter 11 of this book is entirely devoted to creating your own affirmations and Appendix A features a list of sample affirmations.

> *Between stimulus and response, there is a space.*
> *In that space is our power to choose our response.*
> *In our response lies our growth and our freedom.*
> — Stephen Covey

Chapter 2:
Being of Two Minds

The Conscious Mind

When we talk about "thoughts," we're normally referring to thoughts that seem to come from the so-called conscious mind. I say "so-called" because we rarely pay attention to what our thoughts are. Our conscious thoughts are whatever our mind happens to be thinking at any given moment. For example, your conscious mind is reading and understanding these words. Perhaps you've noticed that your conscious mind can only deal with a few things at the same time. You could say the conscious mind is similar to a computer screen that displays whatever you're consciously focusing on.

However, many of us don't fully realize that we have subconscious thoughts as well. As a consequence, the conscious mind rebels against the idea that change can happen without its understanding how or why, and that often makes it hard to change the way we think. The conscious mind wants to change, but it doesn't know how, and sometimes it's reluctant to relinquish control. Since it can't see below the surface, it doesn't realize it's only a small part of the whole.

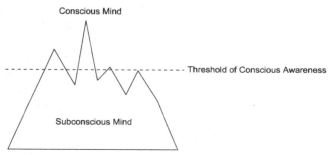

The Subconscious Mind

The subconscious mind encompasses almost everything that's not conscious. Many desires, beliefs and emotions are subconscious, although they're sometimes noticed and expressed consciously. Memories, dreams, daydreams and images, both real and fantastic, live in your subconscious mind. The subconscious is also where your creative resources lie.

Normally, most of the information your conscious mind uses to formulate conscious thought is filed away in the subconscious. Think of your phone number right now. Where was that phone number before I asked you to recall it? It was stored in your subconscious, which is a lot like a computer's database.

Much of the information you receive through your five senses goes directly into the subconscious, allowing only a small proportion to enter the conscious mind. This process prevents the conscious mind from being flooded with sensory information. Whenever you have an experience, your subconscious mind creates and stores a file, sometimes with, and sometimes without, your conscious awareness.

When we were very young children, all our emotions were consciously expressed. However, as we grew older, we quickly learned to control and even suppress emotions and feelings that might be painful or socially unacceptable. At the same time, we may have submerged useful information.

The important thing to remember about your subconscious mind is that it isn't very logical. It's not skilled at telling the difference between an imagined experience and a real one. For example, think of a lemon. In your creative imagination, see, sense and feel a ripe, yellow, juicy lemon. Now imagine taking a knife and cutting open that lemon. Imagine the citrus aroma. Now imagine taking a piece of that lemon and biting into it. Feel the sour juice puckering your mouth and smell the lemony aroma as it floods your nostrils. Close your eyes and focus on imagining the lemon.

If you're like most people, you noticed that your mouth began to salivate as you imagined biting into the lemon. But where is the lemon? It exists solely in your imagination.

Intensity and Repetition

Your subconscious mind learns things in two primary ways: through intensity and repetition. It learns best through a combination of both. One of the reasons you salivated as you bit into an imaginary lemon is that the first time it was an intense experience. You probably can recall some other intense experiences from your life. As you do, notice the way your physiology responds. Think of your first kiss, maybe. Or remember a recent argument and notice that you may be feeling a little more upset than you were before I reminded you.

Repetition works a bit differently. Remember when you learned to drive a car or even earlier when you learned to tie your shoes. When we begin to learn a new and complex skill, we must pay conscious attention to every detail. Remember how awkward it was the first several times? But after a while, the whole process became so *automatic* that now, your conscious mind is barely engaged. Many people have had the experience of driving home and having no conscious memory of how they got there. And most of us can now tie our shoes without even looking!

The key to remember is that once we've learned something to the degree that it's automatic, we no longer think a lot about it. We call such automatic behavior a habit. A habit is often a good thing. However, many of our habits were acquired at a very young age, before we had the full benefit of our education and adult experience. This is one reason we may have trouble succeeding at the things we consciously want to do, such as losing weight, stopping smoking or beginning a fitness program. Consciously, we're determined to do something different, but subconscious habits prevent us.

Not only are we likely to have developed some childish habits of behavior, but we may also have developed habits of thinking that aren't even rational. It's been said that children are excellent perceivers, but terrible interpreters. For example, a child may correctly *perceive* trouble between mom and dad, even though her parents are conscientiously protecting her from their adult concerns. Simultaneously, the child may incorrectly *interpret* that the problem between her parents is somehow her fault. She might even perceive that her parents are keeping a secret from her and interpret that she isn't trustworthy.

The messages you heard repeated by your parents, friends and teachers, the images you see on television and in the movies, and even song lyrics, all combine with your own experiences, interpretations and memories to form a loosely organized, largely subconscious system of beliefs. In a way, we're being hypnotized much of the time. Your belief system engenders emotional and behavioral patterns that can either be beneficial or not. Prospective hypnotherapy clients often ask me, "Do you think I can be hypnotized?" To which I have to stifle the urge to say, "When have you ever *not* been hypnotized?"

Now that we've learned that thoughts are very powerful, can you imagine how important it is to have positive thinking habits? Hypnosis and guided visualization are powerful tools for changing unwanted habits of behavior and thought at the level of the subconscious. In Appendix B of this book, you'll find a guided meditation to help you reprogram your subconscious mind for abundance. If you do nothing else, I suggest you tape yourself reading this meditation. Read the words slowly and listen to the tape on a regular basis. This alone may dramatically change your relationship with abundance.

Chapter 3:
My Story

An Interesting Book

The way I stumbled on how to change my relationship to reality, and to abundance, was accidental. I'd just completed my MFA in painting at UCLA. Eager to spread my artistic wings, I spent much of my time painting, and as always, I was constantly educating myself.

I was very interested in a subject called perceptual psychology, which studies how the brain translates, reconstructs and interprets the things we perceive. As a painter, I was particularly curious about visual perception. It was a practical matter. For instance, how do you paint a white chicken in the shadows? Because the "white" chicken is optically gray, you have to use gray pigment. If you paint it in just the right way, it will be interpreted by the viewer as a white chicken standing in a shadow, not as a gray chicken. There are lots of subliminal perceptual cues that help the brain decide what to perceive. As an artist, I was interested in playing with that edge.

I had a practical interest in the subject, but I was also curious on a deeper level. Not only did I want to learn about how the brain processed sensory data, I also wondered how the mind translates experiences from the outer world into a perceptual inner reality. There was a lot of research being done on this sort of thing in the early '70s.

Luckily there was a nice public library in my neighborhood. I would grab three perceptual psychology books from the shelf, read them, absorb what I needed, return them and then grab the next three. One day, I thought I picked up a book entitled *The Nature of Perceptual Reality*. However, when I got home,

I found I'd actually borrowed the book *The Nature of Personal Reality, A Seth Book,* by Jane Roberts.

As I leafed through its pages, I could see this was not like any other book I'd ever read. Jane Roberts was the author's name according to the cover, but she insisted the true author was a non-physical being named Seth. There is now an entire archive of the Seth material at Yale University, but at the time, I'd never heard of Seth or channeling. My initial reaction was, *These people are crazy. Too weird for me!*

The introduction described how the book had been written. Every Wednesday evening, Jane would sit down on her living room sofa, sip a little wine and go into a trance. Then Seth would speak through Jane and begin dictating his book about personal reality. Meanwhile, Jane's husband, Robert, would record the dictation and ask questions, often getting involved in long discussions with Seth. *Interesting couple*, I thought, not without a touch of sarcasm.

When Jane came out of the trance, she had little or no memory of what Seth had said. However, Seth seemed to have an uncanny memory. He would begin the dictation exactly where he'd left off the previous week. The whole scenario was so outside my definition of normal, I deemed it a "crackpot book" and vowed to take it back to the library as soon as possible, being sure to explain to the librarian that I'd picked up the book by mistake. I didn't want anyone thinking I was a crackpot; certainly not the librarian!

But the introduction had hooked me and I kept reading. Besides, what this Seth guy said was kind of interesting. One of the main things Seth put forward was the concept: you create your own reality. Seth insisted that reality follows your beliefs, not the other way around. Now, this was the most ridiculous idea I'd ever heard. Wasn't it obvious that the experience of reality came first? You experienced reality and then you formed your beliefs based on that experience. That's the way it worked!

As I continued reading, Seth put forth some very interesting and even logical arguments. They got me pondering the nature of reality in ways I'd never thought of before. While driving or walking my dog, I'd sometimes find myself having a deep philosophical discussion with Seth in my mind. I'd have to remind myself that Seth was a self-described non-physical being. *This is ridiculous! I'm arguing with a ghost! There's no such person as Seth! Snap out of it, Linda!*

But Seth's ideas intrigued me and I began to wonder, what if they were true? What if something about my beliefs *was* unconsciously shaping the way I perceived reality? I could see that in some instances it was true—not necessarily 100%, but sometimes. Certainly people from one culture see the world differently than people from another culture. In that way, people's beliefs shape their reality. Perhaps reality was a little more elastic, or at least relative, than I'd ever considered.

One afternoon while reading the book, I thought, *Okay, if I can create my own reality, then let's just prove it.* Larry, my husband at the time, was a busy surgical resident, so a phone call from Larry was a big deal. When he did have a moment to call, it was usually late at night, not in the middle of the afternoon. I had an idea for an experiment. I put the Seth book down in my lap and thought, in a challenging way, *If I can create my own reality, then I say Larry is going to call me right now!*

Rrring! It was instantaneous. I nearly fell off my chair. The instant I'd completed that thought, the phone rang. I picked up the phone and said with confidence, "Hello Larry!" This was in the days before caller ID, so he was very impressed. I tried to explain how I'd known it was him, but he didn't really understand what I was talking about. Perhaps it was just a coincidence, but secretly I celebrated the remarkable results of my little experiment. I was a little giddy with a new sense of power.

My experiment had given me instant feedback. From Larry's point of view, he had a break so he just called, spontaneously. Even telepathy didn't explain what had happened. There hadn't been time for that. No sooner had I finished thinking the thought, when the phone had rung. If I were to believe Seth, I created that phone call. I started opening my mind to the idea that a person's thoughts could influence their reality.

One of the ways Seth said reality could be changed was through conscious intention. I continued experimenting. I practiced setting intentions for things like parking spaces, sometimes successfully and sometimes not. I noticed that my rate of success went down if there were people in the car who doubted we could find a place. If someone said, "We'll never find a parking place," then that person's version of reality was more likely to occur, unless I added more energy into my intention that we *would* find a place. I began to notice that other people's beliefs and attitudes could have an affect on my personal reality too. I noticed that when I spent time with a friend who wasn't very enthusiastic, my own enthusiasm diminished too. When I was with positive energetic people, my energy would increase, and the world would feel full of possibility.

I asked friends if they'd ever heard of the Seth books or channeling, but it was the early '70s and no one had. Very few people were even interested in such things. I didn't take much of it very seriously either and after a while I forgot about Seth.

The Money Seminar

It's hard to imagine now, but in the early '70s, the world of finance was somewhat inaccessible to women. The realm of money was almost entirely male in those days and it was only beginning to change with the feminist movement. I was bright and well educated and I didn't like feeling stupid. I wanted to learn how to deal with money and educate myself about finances, realizing I'd soon have to take more responsibility for them. One day, I received an announcement in the mail about a weekend program for women called The Money Seminar. It caught my eye. The workshop sounded like exactly what I was looking for: how to speak about finances, how to hold your own in a negotiation. It looked very businesslike. I signed up. Fifty bucks. Good investment.

On the morning of the seminar, our teacher, Susan, began to speak about how our thoughts and beliefs create reality. She further explained that most people live within a model of scarcity. We had been taught to believe there's never enough. Not enough love. Not enough money. Not enough of any of the good things in life. In the scarcity model, if I had more, it would mean someone else had less. Even having a little more could make you feel downright selfish and selfish was something we certainly didn't want to be. According to Susan, the universe is like a machine that says yes. "If you believe the universe is abundant, then the universe says yes. If you believe in scarcity, the universe says yes!"

As I listened to Susan speak, I heard her mention several of the principles the Seth book had set out, many of which I'd almost forgotten: "The universe is abundant and we are all children of the universe. Every one of us deserves to be wealthy and prosperous." I was surprised I wasn't learning about tax shelters and mortgage amortization, but I was fascinated by what I was hearing.

During the lunch break, we all sat down in a circle to eat. One of the other women said, "This reminds me of some stuff I read in a strange book. I think it was by a guy named Seth. Have any of you read his book or heard any of these ideas before?"

To this day, the response still gives me chills. As we went around the circle of nearly twenty women, it became clear that every single one of us had read a Seth book. Furthermore, we all had unusual stories to share about how we had happened across the books. It was almost as though by reading the Seth books, we'd been given a certain preparation for the information we were now hearing in the workshop. Not one of us had realized what the class would really be about. Even the people who had written the advertising brochure were unaware it was going to be a metaphysical seminar. The Seth book was like a key in the door of my mind. The key turned and the door began to open.

After the seminar, I started putting some of the principles into practice. I started setting my intention by saying and writing affirmations. Over the years I have learned more about the way thought creates reality. I've manifested money and many other wonderful things using the methods I will teach you in this book.

Moving to Hawaii

By the time Larry completed his surgical residency, it was the early '80s. On our honeymoon in Hawaii, we'd fallen in love with the islands. After visiting Oahu and the outer islands, we chose Kona on the west side of the Big Island of Hawaii as our dream home. I began making affirmations that our family could move to Kona and Larry would start his surgical practice there.

At first, the whole idea didn't seem very realistic. For one thing, the economy was in recession. In those days, it was almost impossible for doctors from the mainland to get licensed to practice in Hawaii. Even if Larry could get his Hawaiian medical license, the small population of West Hawaii was barely enough to keep one or two general surgeons busy. A quick check of the Kona phonebook revealed there were already seven in town. It appeared there was no room for us. To add to the drama, I had a new baby son and I was pregnant. But I'd learned that intention is a powerful tool.

This is what I did. Every afternoon for several weeks, I put my baby in a backpack and walked round and round the track at our neighborhood high school, saying affirmations to myself and visualizing my new life in Hawaii. I visualized a home, an office, Larry's practice full and thriving, and a healthy, happy environment for my family and me.

Because I was pregnant, we needed to decide whether I'd give birth to my baby before or after we moved to Kona. On one of our preliminary trips, we scheduled a prenatal visit with an obstetrics group on the Big Island, in order to evaluate the quality of available medical care. To my surprise, the doctors were great. They had excellent training and because of the small-town atmosphere, had time to really get to know their patients. I remembered the impersonal quality of the medical care I'd received at the large city hospital where I'd given birth to my first son. I knew in my heart that I wanted my baby to be born in Kona.

During that appointment, Larry had a friendly chat with the doctor. He was very impressed with Larry's credentials and, to our surprise, encouraged us to move there. He explained why. Since all the general surgeons in Kona were hungry for business, they had turned to doing general practice in addition to surgery. This did not go over well with the local internists, ob-gyns and family practitioners. Consequently, the non-surgeons had been quietly referring patients who needed elective surgery to hospitals in Honolulu on Oahu. It seemed a turf war was raging in paradise.

Larry was strictly interested in surgery. He assured the obstetrician that he had no interest whatsoever in general practice. "In that case," the doctor said, "considering your credentials, we'd love to send our elective surgery to you so our patients can have their operations done here at Kona Hospital." The doctor gave us the names of a few other Kona physicians who might also be interested in referring surgical patients to Larry. At that moment, we realized there actually was a patient base for

Larry's practice—it had just been hidden. Before we left, the doctor told us a recent court case had made the licensing problem disappear. If a doctor passed his National Board Exam, the State of Hawaii had to approve the license. Since Larry had already passed his boards, all he needed was a little paper work and the fee.

The universe had certainly given us a green light, but there was still more to create. We needed money for moving expenses, to finance a new home and to set up a new surgery office. Larry started moonlighting in the Emergency Room on weekends which helped, but I was the pregnant mother of a toddler. It didn't make sense for me to work. We saved, but it wasn't enough. We had no idea where the extra money was going to come from, especially if we moved to Kona before the birth of our new baby. However, I kept setting my intention, saying my affirmations and holding the vision of our new life in Hawaii.

One morning, Larry received an official-looking letter in the mail. Larry's dad had been a free spirit who had lived out his last years very simply. When he had died the year before, we assumed he'd left no estate. To our surprise, the letter stated there was an inheritance of $30,000, to be divided equally among the three surviving children. We spent Larry's $10,000 on medical equipment and furniture for his office-to-be. A few months later, Larry's brother loaned us his part of the inheritance to help pay our bills while we got started in Kona and which we soon paid back.

The necessary money had arrived, as it was needed, seemingly out of the blue. No one even knew it existed. Perhaps it was luck or even grace. I believe a large part of our success was because of intention. I had paved the way by writing and saying affirmations, which cleared the inner obstacles and doubts, allowing for greater possibilities than at first seemed "realistic."

Financial Freedom

Having learned these concepts, and having practiced them over time, I can say I've experienced financial freedom in my life since then. By financial freedom, I don't necessarily mean having millions in the bank. To me, financial freedom means never having to do something I don't like just for the money and never having to say no to something I really want to do for lack of money.

I've done many things people tell themselves they can't. I moved to Hawaii and I moved away from Hawaii. I have traveled to Europe several times. At fifty, I took off for a couple of years on a cross-country adventure, traveling around North America in an RV with my sweetheart Chris (Larry and I divorced in 1994).

During that trip, we met a lot of people on the road who said, "That's the life. I'd love to do that someday." We'd ask, "Well, why don't you? What are you waiting for? You know someday never comes!" Usually, the answer was, "Oh, I can't afford it, you know?" or "Somebody has to pay the rent!"

If you are living from the belief that abundance will serve and support you, you can actually let go of your home base and travel for two or three years, even at an age when most people are settling down for the long haul. Abundance will support you if you allow it to. Leandra Carroll writes about this beautifully in her wonderful book, *The Architecture of All Abundance*. She calls it "living on the wind."

During our time on the road, Chris and I rarely knew where we would be sleeping each night. We didn't focus on how it would work out, we just trusted that it would. Letting go of the "how" led to some happy surprises. Sure, we camped in Wal-Mart parking lots, but sometimes we lived in mansions. For instance, we spent three months house-sitting multimillion-dollar houses on Hilton Head Island living in opulence for free, and in some cases even getting paid. Of course we had a working plan, but it was very flexible and usually we just followed our noses. It's fine to have a plan, as long as that plan includes an openness to abundance, thus stacking the deck in your favor.

As I've said, financial freedom for me doesn't necessarily mean having a ton of money in the bank. It means freedom from financial restrictions. Financial freedom can manifest in many wonderful and interesting ways, in addition to money. I tell you truthfully, I've met more than one millionaire who did not feel financially free. Unless you are willing to accept the *experience* of abundance, no amount of money will make you feel secure and happy. Money can't buy that.

For much of my life, many amazing things have seemingly just fallen into place. For the record, I want you to know that I've always felt a Divine presence guiding me in my life. For me, affirmations, intention and visualization are a form of prayer, a way of surrendering my will to Divine Will. However, you don't have to believe in Divine Will for these principles to work in your life. The "how" of it may not make sense now, but when you do the affirmation work, you are plugging into the flow of the abundant universe and saying "yes!"

Chapter 4:
Belief Creates Reality

Reality is merely an illusion, albeit a very persistent one.
—Albert Einstein

For our purposes, let's define a belief as a loosely organized structure of thoughts and emotions. Sometimes a belief is dominated by emotion, in which case we may experience emotional upset if that belief is challenged. When speaking about our emotional beliefs, we often use the verb "feel." Some beliefs are more intellectual. When we speak about our intellectual beliefs, we tend to use the verb "think." When an intellectual belief is challenged, we tend to be argumentative or dismissive, discounting evidence contrary to our existing belief.

Everyone has some beliefs that are invisible. Because they are invisible, we don't label them as beliefs; we're convinced That's The Way Things Are. I call such beliefs "core beliefs". They can be dangerous if left unexamined, because they have the strongest influence on our experience of reality. Core beliefs have such a hold on our consciousness, that we may be unable to perceive the unlimited possibilities available to us in any given moment.

We will act consistently with our view of who we truly are,
whether that view is accurate or not.

—Anthony Robbins

I understand that you may not believe me just yet. But perhaps you can just imagine for the time being that the following statements are true: Your thoughts create your emotions.

Your emotions, together with your thoughts, generate actions. Actions generate results.

Thoughts ⟶ Emotions ⟶ Actions ⟶ Results

Most of the time, when people want to know what's "real", they look at their outer results. Outer results exist in the physical world and are therefore easier to experience as "reality." Actually, it's more accurate to say that our experience of reality is our perception of results combined with our response to those results. The quality of your results, and therefore your reality, is absolutely relative to the quality of your beliefs. Something a person believes to be a hard fact of reality is often nothing more than a favorite core belief, undefined as such. Remember, it was once a "reality" that the world was flat and that the sun circled the earth. Anyone who believed differently was ridiculed or even tortured.

As we go through life, we generate a kind of feedback loop. Our beliefs create actions, which create results. Then we judge our results as good or bad and those judgments are thoughts and emotions which feed back into our beliefs and so on. It's an automatic cycle which creates a strong impression that our beliefs are being formed by "reality." It's true that our results are a part of reality, but it's not true that they're the cause of our reality. That's why we call them results!

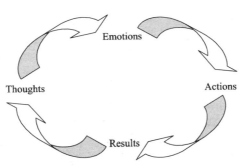

The Upward Spiral

Pete and Joe each started a business. Both invested a lot of time and energy. Both were optimistic. Both took a lot of positive actions and worked hard. In Pete's case, the business failed. Of course, Pete wasn't pleased with his results, and like many people, he began to experience self-doubt. He thought, *I'm a failure*, *I'm unlucky with money*, *I can't seem to succeed even though I work hard*, or even *I'm ruined!* Pete's in danger of falling into a downward spiral. He begins unconsciously reinforcing the "reality" of failure with negative thoughts. Pete feels depressed and unenergetic. At this point, he's "right" about not being able to attract much success.

On the other hand, Joe's business succeeded. He's delighted with the results and it shows. He feels great about his life and is ready for more. He has an "I can do it!" attitude. Joe has entered the upward spiral, because his thoughts are now reinforcing the "reality" of his success. Even if Joe experiences a failure, it's unlikely to affect his attitude for long. Of course he'll be disappointed, but he'll also be curious about what happened and how he can learn from his mistakes. Unlike Pete, "failure" is feedback for Joe, not a life sentence.

Henry Ford said, "There are two kinds of people. Those who think they can, and those who think they can't, and they are both right." The truth is, Joe and Pete aren't that different. Like most of us, they've learned to experience "reality" based almost solely on past results. Neither has learned the tremendous power of Intention to shape results. Joe's success has influenced his thoughts and how those thoughts support his success. Pete is focusing on a reality he doesn't want. However, with intention, Pete could consciously focus on the reality he wants to create, rather than focusing on the reality he doesn't want. By consciously focusing on the reality he would like to create, Pete could harness the energy of the upward spiral to activate and magnetize the success he desires.

To Change Your Results, Change Your Thoughts

Most of us, whether successful or unsuccessful, typically fix our attention on our results. Rarely do we examine the thoughts and emotions which are creating those results. This is especially true when it comes to abundance. We imagine that forces beyond our control determine our relationship to abundance. If you've never taken the time to examine your beliefs about abundance, this book will give you the opportunity to do so. You'll discover whether or not your beliefs are helping you create a happy life full of abundance.

If you don't realize that your actions are determined by your beliefs, you may wonder why you haven't been able to create the life you want. Let's take the example of Karen.

One day, Karen looked in the mirror and didn't like what she saw. She hadn't had a date in a while and believed the place to start was to improve her appearance. She'd gained a little weight, but didn't like to exercise. Karen frowned and made a resolution: *Tomorrow, I'm going to start going to the gym everyday to work out.*

But the next day, instead of getting up early and heading to the gym, Karen watched the morning news on TV and for breakfast, she ate a donut in the car on the way to work. Then she remembered her resolution and judged herself harshly. *No wonder no one loves me*, she thought. *Not only am I fat and ugly, I have no self-control either.* Karen felt depressed, hopeless and guilty. Wanting to feel better, she reached for a second donut.

If Karen examined her beliefs, she would discover that her decision to go to the gym was based on self-loathing because she believes she isn't okay. Looking deeper, Karen might find she has quite a few beliefs that aren't helping her. She believes she's not good enough. She also believes love is scarce and only beautiful people deserve to be loved. As a child, Karen's parents often gave the kids sweets for a treat. Now Karen believes a sweet, gooey treat will cheer her up when she's feeling low. No wonder she goes for the donuts rather than to the gym!

As long as Karen has a belief that she isn't worthy of love, it will be difficult for her to generate actions that are self-loving. Even if Karen finds a mate who loves her, she will doubt that love as long as she has the core belief that she's unlovable unless she's perfect. There will always be a fearful part of Karen believing that if her partner knew the truth about her, he would reject her.

Karen has it backwards. She believes that if she could be perfect, then and only then, will she deserve love. The truth is, if Karen started believing she deserves love, just as she is, then taking good care of her body would come naturally. Perhaps that would mean going to the gym regularly. Or it might mean taking long walks in Nature, eating healthy organic food, learning to belly dance, taking a more active job or any number of things. If Karen believes she deserves love, her range of options is much wider than choosing between donuts or the gym. When Karen feels deserving, her choices are based on doing things she loves.

When it comes to creating a life that we love, most of us don't even have an idea where the "gym" is. We don't know where to go or what to do. I'm saying that the "gym" is in your mind; that you need to exercise more resourceful thoughts. Not only will you feel better mentally and physically, your actions are more likely to lead to positive results. And that's more likely to get you in the upward spiral.

To reiterate, thoughts and emotions drive your actions, and your actions create results. The reason we believe reality creates our beliefs is that after we get results, those results start driving our thoughts. There's a circuit. Remember, it's easiest to interrupt a negative cycle at the level of thought. At the level of thought, a small change can create a dramatically different result.

Here's an analogy. Imagine you're the captain of a ship setting sail from Hawaii to San Francisco. On this imaginary journey, your thoughts are the ship's rudder. Your positive thoughts keep you on course, but your negative thoughts take you off course. Let's say you have a negative thought and begin heading to Vancouver. Vancouver's a fine destination, but you've selected San Francisco as your goal for this trip.

You have a negative thought and begin to wander off course. As soon as you do, you begin thinking, *Oh, no! I'm so stupid! What's wrong with me? Nothing ever goes my way.* Now, this isn't very resourceful thinking for any ship's captain, imaginary or real! As you continue indulging in negative thoughts, berating yourself and cursing the gods, you are now well on your way to Alaska! But whenever you think positively, you're once again heading toward San Francisco. In fact, the more positive your thoughts, the faster you'll get to your desired destination. The swiftest way to end up in San Francisco is to adjust and continue thinking positive thoughts, correcting your course often and as soon as possible. If you try to change course when you've already arrived in Vancouver, you've got a much longer journey to make.

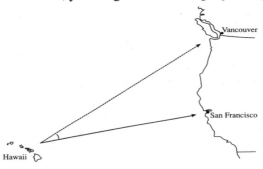

Small changes can create big differences in destination. If you're going to make an interception in your life, begin with your thoughts. That's the most powerful place you can make changes in your results and therefore your reality. Remember that your actions are generated by your thoughts, so if you change your thoughts, your actions will tend to follow automatically.

It's been said that a typical commercial airliner is off course ninety percent of the time, yet it usually arrives at its destination because the navigator makes many corrections along the way. Your thoughts are your navigational system. Where would you like them to take you?

It is not in the stars to hold our destiny, but in ourselves.
—William Shakespeare

Complaining Keeps Things Stuck

A complaint is a negative statement about a reality you don't like. It's especially dangerous, because we tend to feel just a little bit self-righteous when we're complaining. The Little Voice has a field day! Everything you complain about may be true, but your complaining is feeding energy into that which you *don't* want. Your complaints are holding the unwanted pattern and reinforcing that undesirable reality.

In 1999, when Chris and I started on our road trip together, we had some adjustments to make. We're both independent and very different in how we do things. Now we were spending long hours together in close quarters, often in stressful conditions. The ways Chris solved problems frequently threatened my comfort zone. Soon, I began to find fault and complain to Chris about everything I felt he was doing "wrong."

Like most people, I was convinced that the only way I could change what I didn't like was to let Chris know, in detail, what I didn't like and why I didn't like it. I couldn't understand why he didn't just get with the program. My program. But Chris is a Taurus and stubborn. He didn't change and I found myself repeating the same complaints, until even I couldn't stand the sound of myself.

Then, in the middle of an argument, I had a moment of clarity. I remembered what I teach and decided to put it to the test. I decided to go on a fast—a complaint fast. As hard as it was, I made a vow to stop complaining. It wasn't easy. At first, I just bit my tongue and complained in my mind instead of out loud. Sometimes, I'd sneak one in by smiling and saying, "Darling, this isn't a complaint, it's just a simple *observation* that you're going ten miles over the speed limit." After a while, my mind settled down and I'd simply hold a positive thought of how I'd like things to be, without thinking anything negative toward Chris. Within a couple of weeks, nearly every problem I'd been complaining about, simply disappeared! It was amazing. The paradox is that when things are going wrong, it's not the time to complain; it's the time to break the negative circuit by stating an affirmation toward what you *do* want.

Even though I know this is possible, I often find myself stuck in the old pattern. I now believe that complaining is an addiction, as powerful and destructive as any drug. There ought to be a twelve-step program for Complainers Anonymous and their close relatives, Faultfinders Anonymous. You know who you are!

Let's say you believe you're unappreciated at work and that you never get a promotion or raise. Your belief will tend to hold that reality in place. Complaining will further perpetuate the problem. To create a new reality, start by changing your thoughts. The thought: *People value and honor my work*, would send your energy out into the world in a different, more positive way. Repeat to yourself twenty times every morning for twenty-one days, *People value and honor my work*. You will be amazed at the results. Even if you feel weird saying it, you'll begin to carry yourself differently. Other people's reactions to you will begin to change, even though you haven't said a word to them. Your boss may change, or you may change bosses! Either way, you'll be much more likely to end up in a place where your work is valued and honored if you're holding that thought.

Chapter 5
Filters

While I can't entirely explain why the outer world follows the inner world, one concept that helps our understanding is the idea of perceptual filters.

Filter Exercise:

Important: Do not read ahead until you have finished the first part of this exercise!

Take a minute to look around the room you're in. Notice the blue things in the room and write them down quickly.

1. _____

2. _____

3. _____

4. _____

5. _____

6. _____

7. _____

8. _____

Now, close your eyes and *without* looking, list all the red things in the room.

1. _____

2. _____

3. _____

4. _____

5. _____

6. _____

7. _____

8. _____

When you've finished your list, then and only then, take a look around the room and notice the number of red things you failed to see when you were looking for blue things. When you have a filter for blue, red doesn't enter your awareness very easily.

That's why it's important to be aware of your filters. If your filter is always looking for problems, what solutions are you blocking out?

As evolving conscious beings, we exist in a field of possibilities, but we put limits on what we can and can't do. Our beliefs become filters through which we perceive only a few choices within the enormous possibilities available at any given moment. Our beliefs can filter out the very solutions to our problems, until we become stuck in a rut we believe we can't get out of.

Filters are the lenses we see reality through, but we're not generally aware of them. If you make the case that there's not enough to go around, then you experience the world through that lens and find plenty of evidence supporting that belief. However, if you make the case that there's plenty to go around, you'll find plenty of evidence supporting that too. In either example, your filter influences your awareness of alternative possibilities.

In his book *Prometheus Rising*, Robert Anton Wilson suggests you visualize a quarter vividly for a minute, then take a walk down the street while continuing to visualize the quarter. Chances are, you'll find a quarter before long.

Similarly, I saw some US Sacagawea one-dollar coins being sold on television. I hadn't realized they'd become collectible and mentioned to Chris that we should find the few we had lying around the house and take better care of them. Two days later, as Chris pulled the loose change from his pocket he discovered a shiny new golden Sacagawea coin someone had given him as change by mistake.

Have you ever decided to buy a certain model car, then all of a sudden you see that model everywhere? Were they there before? Perhaps, but once that filter's in place, they start popping out of the landscape.

Once you realize that you have filters, you may want to hose them off or perhaps change them. At least you'll become aware that there may be many more possibilities in life than your filters are letting you see. Filters tend to distort the way we view the world. In order to have clear vision, we need good, clear lenses. Even with clear lenses, we have to keep them clean. It's an ongoing practice, like washing dishes or making the bed.

Undiscovered Possibilities

The other day, I was walking behind a man on the street. He looked like he might be homeless. For some reason, I sensed there was something I could learn from him. I soon observed that every time he walked past a payphone, he habitually checked to see if there was a quarter in the coin return slot. And every time he went by the trash, he quickly checked to see if anything of value had been thrown away.

His filter was really interesting. He was looking for things that other people had overlooked. That's not a bad filter to have. However, the man was severely limiting himself by looking for quarters and trash. Even on a good day, all he's going to find is quarters and trash. His model was too small.

It's actually quite a beneficial thing to have the mindset of looking for something valuable that others may have missed. Many astute people have become wealthy with just such a mindset. I met a woman who created a thriving business by simply auditing shipping charges for large mail-order companies. She finds so many unnoticed errors that she earns a six-figure income splitting the refunds with the companies who use her service. Another friend began collecting tons of discarded macadamia nut husks from orchards in Hawaii. The farmers were happy when he offered to haul them away. He's made a small fortune reselling the husks as fertile compost. The idea for Velcro came from noticing the way certain seeds stick to your socks. There are many things people throw in the trash that are valuable, but most of them are possibilities, not things. There are undiscovered million-dollar ideas everywhere that haven't been noticed yet.

The universe is full of magical things patiently waiting
for our wits to grow sharper.

—Eden Phillpotts

Fun in the Sun and Income Too

My mother, Wanita Holmes, is also a hypnotherapist. When I still lived in Hawaii, my mother used to resist coming to visit because, as a self-employed hypnotherapist, she would miss a week of work and therefore a week's income. She'd say, "I don't want to lose the work." I'd reassure her, "You're not losing the work; you're just rescheduling it."

While my mother had a strong belief that if she took time off she'd lose money, she also knew the power of her thoughts. She started affirming, "I am not losing work, I am just rescheduling it." She also started affirming that she deserved to take time off. She even opened her mind a little to the idea that there might be a way she could earn money while vacationing in Hawaii.

The next time Mom visited, she got a great package deal, giving her hotel accommodation and airfare for less than the price of regular airfare. Even though she usually stayed with us, she decided to take the package and use the hotel room, so the whole family could enjoy the hotel pool and beach.

As it happened, and unbeknownst to Mom, Tad James was conducting a Master Neurolinguistic Programming training for hypnotherapists at the very same hotel. Many of the trainees had flown in from California for the weekend. As Mom was lounging by the pool, she recognized several familiar faces among the crowd coming from the Grand Ballroom during a break. Many of them came over to say hello, because my mother is very well known in the California hypnotherapy community. Some of them were smoking. One of the things my mother is well known for is her talent for helping people become non-smokers. She teased her cigarette-smoking colleagues and told them they'd better come to see her soon. They agreed and she quickly booked four appointments while sitting by the pool! Moreover, those sessions were so successful, that the hypnotherapists later enrolled in her seminar to learn the hypnosis method she'd used. Mom ended up making thousands of dollars more than if she'd stayed home.

That's how easily it can happen. If you start letting go of your need to know *how* abundance is going to come, you connect to a larger potential than you could possibly imagine and things start to change. It's that simple.

Today the greatest single source of wealth is between your ears.
                                                            —Brian Tracy

Chapter 6:
What is Abundance?

Define Abundance

Before I tell you my views on abundance, I invite you to quickly write your own definition of abundance below.

_____

_____

_____

_____

_____

_____

   Perhaps your definition includes having a lot of money and other things. When people hear "abundance," they often tend to think in terms of material things.

   I'm going to suggest that abundance isn't about *having* things. I believe that abundance is actually a state of consciousness. Abundance is a way of thinking, an attitude and a way of being. Abundance is a quality, not a quantity. As Wayne Dyer says, "Abundance is not something we acquire. It is something we tune into."

Abundance is Flow

Do you know what the word *abundance* means, if you look up its derivation? *Abundance* has two parts: *ab*, which means, "move away from," and *unda*, which means, "wave." Literally, abundance means moving outward in a wave. Look in a good dictionary and you'll find that many words having to do with money or wealth involve images of water and the idea of *flow*. *Flow* is embedded in the language of abundance and wealth. For example, the word *wealth* comes from the word *well*, which is also related to the word *wave*. Another term for money is *currency* which is derived from *current* meaning running or flowing. We also use the word current to describe the movement of water, electricity and even time.

My friend Tina used to be a world-class windsurfer. She'd tell me, "I don't surf on the water. I surf on the energy moving *through* the water." Abundance is a current of energy. It's like the wave flowing through the water. Having an abundant life, requires having a good relationship with the flow of abundance.

Without energy moving through it, water is likely to become stagnant and polluted. Fresh water means flowing water. However, too much energy moving too quickly can result in a flood. So when I use the word abundance in this book, I'm speaking of a continuous, life-sustaining flow of good things into and through your life. Abundance is not about amassing and hoarding great numbers of dollars or material things. It's a healthy, nourishing flow that sustains you with all that you need.

In order to be useful, energy has to flow. This is true in wealth, in health or even electricity. When you switch on the lights in your house, you're allowing the current to flow. Rich people don't just have money; they circulate it and they're skilled at doing so. One way to think of money is as the lifeblood of a project or business.

In order to live within the flow of abundance, you have to get your energy flowing. You may be surprised to find that one of the best ways to start receiving greater abundance is to give away abundance, but more about that later.

Two Models of the Universe

When I say "the universe," I'm talking about everything that affects your life. Your personal universe is much smaller than the cosmos, yet it contains a vast expanse of personal experience and information. In an effort to make sense, your mind constructs a simplified model that's easier to grasp. Having a model can be a useful way to test out ideas. The disadvantage is that if your mental model isn't resourceful, it can work against you instead of helping you.

Most of us have been taught a scarcity model of the universe. From childhood on we're constantly bombarded with messages of scarcity: "money doesn't grow on trees," "it's a dog-eat-dog world." The mentality of scarcity generates fear, greed and negative competition. The scarcity model says that if you have something, less is available for everyone else. When you live in the world of scarcity, there will never be enough money or stuff to make you feel secure.

But what if scarcity, like abundance, is simply a state of mind? What if we imagine instead, an infinitely abundant universe? When you choose the model of abundance, security doesn't come from having the biggest slice of the pie. It comes from knowing that no matter how often you bathe in the sun's rays, you can return to them again and again, without affecting anyone else's ability to do the same. That's an abundant model of the universe.

Acknowledge Abundance

One way to shift your paradigm to the model of abundance is to acknowledge the abundance you have right now. Rather than trying to control the outer world, let's begin with your inner world.

Make a list of your positive qualities, aspects of yourself that you have in abundance. Your warmth, for example, or your compassion. Your humor, smile, intelligence, friendship, your ability to grow and learn. Whatever positive qualities you have in abundance.

1. _____

2. _____

3. _____

4. _____

5. _____

6. _____

7. _____

8. _____

9. _____

10. _____

Next, take five minutes to list some of the many things you have in abundance right now. List anything you have an unlimited supply of. For example, you can always tune into a radio station or you can always take another breath of air. How many seconds have you been alive? Celebrate the abundance you already have flowing through your life.

1. _____

2. _____

3. _____

4. _____

5. _____

6. _____

7. _____

8. _____

9. _____

10. _____

How did you do? If it was easy for you to make these lists, you are well on your way to shifting into the abundant model of the universe. When you refocus your awareness away from problems and toward the positive aspects of your life, you feel better and the positive will automatically increase. However, if this exercise was challenging, pay close attention to the next section.

An Attitude of Gratitude

Gratitude alone can change your life. Oprah Winfrey suggests that people cultivate an attitude of gratitude. She has kept a gratitude journal for years in which she writes down four new things she's grateful for every day. How do you think this affects her outlook on the world? Would you say Oprah has an abundant life? She's learned this powerful secret: the more you say "thank you," the more you will have to appreciate.

When you are grateful, fear disappears and abundance appears.
—Anthony Robbins

List at least ten things you're grateful for. Things you appreciate or that give you pleasure, such as a beautiful sunset, jazz, great food, a helping hand, a child's smile, *The Simpsons,* the song of a bird, the fragrance of a rose. You get the idea.

1. _____

2. _____

3. _____

4. _____

5. _____

6. _____

7. _____

8. _____

9. _____

10. _____

Flowing Abundance

One of the simplest and most effective ways to increase the flow of abundance into your life is to affirm abundance by giving something away freely. It doesn't have to be money, although tithing is a long-honored tradition. Tithing is when you give away a portion of all you earn, usually ten percent, to a good cause. Many people who tithe have noticed that when they tithe, their abundance increases, as if by magic. If you have money, consider giving a little away to get the flow going. Tithing affirms the flow of abundance. At the same time, it affirms that you're not just a receiver, but also a channel through which abundance flows.

The Journey of a Dollar

In the scarcity universe, paying bills isn't fun and it's often painful. In the abundant universe, paying bills is an opportunity to create flow. Imagine you're letting out the old to make space for the new. When you pay your bills, practice saying to yourself: "The money I spend comes back to me multiplied."

If you could follow the journey of one single dollar, you would be amazed at how far and wide it travels. When you pay your phone bill, do you think the phone company holds onto your money forever? No, they spend, loan or invest it in all kinds of projects. When you pay your bills, don't think of it as money going down the drain. Imagine your money circulating in the world, enhancing and blessing everyone whose life it touches.

Some people reading this book might be thinking they have nothing but a lot of debt. I've heard people say that they won't feel financially free until they're completely out of debt. It's helpful to remember that your debt represents other people's confidence in your ability to pay the money back, and with interest. Why argue with their high opinion of you? A good affirmation for dealing with debt is, "My income now greatly exceeds my outflow."

By the way, wealthy people borrow money too. But they tend to borrow money that will generate more money. They use credit cards for convenience or to accrue frequent flier rewards, knowing they'll pay the total balance every month. They borrow money as an investment, not for impulse purchases or survival. Perhaps you are in a survival situation right now and feel you just don't have any money to give. But, whether or not you have money, there's so much more that you can give. For example you can give enthusiasm. Give your energy to things that make you happy. Give your time, energy or attention to those people or situations that need it.

The Golden Rule

The Golden Rule says to do unto others as you would have them do unto you. The reason it's a golden rule is that it's a pathway to real treasure. If you want more love, give love. If you want more support, give support to others. If you want more joy, smile more often. If you want to feel appreciated, tell someone how much you appreciate them. Give away the things you would like to increase in your life. As you do, you'll begin shifting your focus, so that instead of waiting for good things to come to you, you experience yourself as the *source* of good things. That is a powerful feeling.

One of the magical things about unconditional love, compassion or goodwill is that you can't give it away without feeling it yourself. It's a sort of "two for the price of one" deal. Neale Donald Walsch says, "If you decide to give abundantly of all the magic that lies within you, the magic that lies outside of you will be attracted to you and become as much a part of you as you allow it to become."

Ten things you can give away right now

List ten things you could give away abundantly right now—not *should* or *would* give away, but *could*. For example you could give away abundant smiles, compliments or gratitude. If you gave away just these three things, people would want to be around you and they wouldn't even know why. They'd want to give you all kinds of good things too.

1. _____

2. _____

3. _____

4. _____

5. _____

6. _____

7. _____

8. _____

9. _____

10. _____

Start celebrating and sharing abundance on a daily basis and watch your life change before your eyes.

Chapter 7:
The Power of Your Word

In the beginning was the Word.

—Genesis 1:1

If your thoughts create reality, then your *words* are even more powerful. This is because words are the first step toward manifesting thought into physical form. Perhaps an inspiration comes to your mind in the form of a thought. Initially, you may experience this thought as little more than a feeling. When you are ready to make the inspiration more real, you begin to formulate the idea into words or an image.

A thought can stay as a thought forever, until you put it into words. It doesn't matter whether these are inner words or outer words, your words have the power to influence your life and the world. Words can create and words can destroy. When you express those inner words as speech or writing, they have even greater power.

The Power of a Single Word

As a hypnotherapist, my mother Wanita Holmes is also my colleague. One day, a client—we'll call him Fred—came in, bemoaning his life. He had no money for the rent, his car was about to be repossessed and his girlfriend had dumped him. His complaining went on for twenty minutes.

My mother encouraged Fred to shift his thoughts toward what was possible, rather than what had happened in the past. He resisted. Exasperated, she asked, "Isn't there *anything* good happening in your life?"

He hung his head and quietly replied, "No."

She argued gently, giving him a list of things he had going for him: his reasonably good looks, his health and his expertise with computers. He agreed, though reluctantly. While it was true he was skilled with computers, he hadn't had much business recently.

My mother described to him how the power of a single word could transform his life. "It says in the Bible, 'As a man thinketh, so he is,'" she said. "It also says 'In the beginning was the Word' and 'The word became flesh.' Fred, what you say becomes reality."

She asked him to repeat the word *abundance* aloud several times. At first he barely muttered, "Abundance."

"You can do better than that. Say it louder!" she insisted.

"Abundance," he said, still reluctant.

"I mean really loud and with some enthusiasm!"

Fred squirmed in his chair, "Oh, all right. Abundance!"

Clearly uncomfortable with the exercise, Fred tried to change the subject. "Hey, where does it say that stuff in the Bible?" he asked.

"I'm not sure," answered my mom. "I haven't looked it up in quite a while."

Fred started fumbling in his backpack, "Because I have the Bible on this CD."

My mother was amazed. "You mean they've put the whole Bible on that little disc?"

"Yes," said Fred, "and we could search it to find those quotes in an instant, if you had a computer."

"Well, Mary has one and she's in the office next door. Let's go see if we can use it."

Relieved to get out of the spotlight, Fred gladly followed my mother to Mary's office. But when they got there, Mary was hunched over her keyboard looking confused. When she heard the request she said, "I'd love to help, but I'm doing a system upgrade and I'm having some problems." My mother explained that Fred was a computer expert. Mary was thrilled and asked Fred how much he would charge to help her out. He agreed to do it for $300. She hired him instantly.

While Fred began working on the computer, Mary phoned her husband. He owned a business that wanted to do the same upgrade, so he decided to hire Fred too. By that time, the next client had wandered into Mary's office looking for my mother and noticed Fred working on Mary's computer. She mentioned that she had a problem with her computer at home and asked Fred if he made house calls. He said yes and she hired him on the spot.

The results were no less than amazing. Even though he hadn't been in the mood to try, after briefly concentrating on the word *abundance*, Fred had created more than $1200 worth of business in ten minutes.

What Are You Sentencing Yourself To?

When a new client comes to me they often say, "I'm sick and tired" of some problem, or such and such is "a pain in the neck."

I stop them immediately. "Time out! Your subconscious just heard you say that. Your subconscious is very literal. If it hears you repeat that message enough times, it's likely to create the reality that you are sick and tired or that you actually do have pain in your neck."

When you use such seemingly harmless figures of speech, or when you complain "I never _____" or "I always _____," you may literally be *sentencing* yourself to your problems. Or perhaps you're in the habit of sentencing someone else by complaining, "you always_____" or "you never _____." Let me be clear: Using such language actually helps keep those unwanted situations in place. That's the bad news.

The good news is, you can also use the power of language to change the situation. One of the primary purposes of this book is to give you a new language. "Always" and "never" are both a long, long time. Do you really want to *sentence* yourself to something negative for a lifetime? Save these potent words for positive things you want to create and manifest, such as, "I always have plenty of money," or "I never miss a great opportunity." Always and never are two favorite words of The Little Voice, especially when it's complaining. Remember, we want to train The Little Voice to be more resourceful. Here's a trick. Whenever you catch yourself thinking or saying always or never in a negative way, try inserting these three little words: "up until now."

For example:

Change: "I'm never lucky in love."
To: *"Up until now*, I've never been lucky in love."

Change: "I always have problems finding a job that pays well."
To: *"Up until now*, I've always had a problem finding a job that pays well."

Notice how those three little words seem to unlock a world of possibilities?

Chapter 8:
Money: The Most Creative Act
of the Human Imagination

*Only when the last tree has died and the last river has been
poisoned and the last fish been caught will we realize
we cannot eat money.*

—Cree Indian Proverb

What is Money?

Sometimes, money seems to be the most "real" thing in the world. Actually, money only has value because human beings declare that it does. Whether in the form of precious metals or ink on paper, money, in and of itself, has no value. As the Cree proverb says, you can't eat it. Well, you can, but it wouldn't nourish you. Money won't shelter you and it won't keep you warm unless you burn it.

Now that the world has turned to plastic and cyberspace, money is more clearly than ever a form of *energy*. That's all money is: a symbol of human energy and imagination. Money isn't good or bad unless you say it is. Perhaps the reason money is so powerful is that it has unlimited potential. It has no intention, other than the one you give it. Money is ultimately a thought.

If money is a symbol of energy, another way to think of it is like a mirror that reflects how you are managing your personal energy. Your relationship with money will tend to be influenced by what you believe about your personal power in the world. Where does your energy go? Is it leaking? Is it increasing? Your bank balance can give you a very honest, if sometimes uncomfortable, accounting.

When it comes to abundance, many people are stuck on money. Perhaps you feel that abundance is okay, but money isn't. Perhaps you believe that money is intrinsically bad, dirty or evil. Perhaps you learned from your family that money causes conflict. All of us have been bombarded with lots of confusing and contradictory images of money and wealthy people in the media.

I repeat, money is not anything, in and of itself, unless you label it. And you can choose or change your label. Remember, money is only a symbol.

If you want to change your relationship to money, first you need to examine what you truly believe about it. How are your beliefs about money working for you? Are they beneficial or not? Are they even rational or consistent?

In this chapter, you'll have the opportunity to explore some of the conscious, and unconscious, notions you have about money and wealth. You will be doing a series of simple exercises designed to find out what you believe about money, perhaps without even realizing it. You'll find out which of these beliefs are helpful, and which may be stopping you from having a more positive relationship with money and abundance. Some of your responses might surprise you.

As you do the exercises don't censor yourself, but quickly and honestly write down everything you can think of off the top of your head. This is not the time to be politically correct. Just keep free-associating and let it all come out. No one else but you needs to see what you write. You can photocopy the pages or write your answers in a notebook. And you can even burn them after you're done. Oddly enough, most of us feel more comfortable talking about sex than we do talking about our relationship with money. That tells you something right there.

What are your thoughts about money?

Quickly complete the statement: "Money is _____."
Keep going until you can't think of anything else to say and then say a few more things. If you have more than ten, good. Keep writing. Take no more than two or three minutes. We want your snap judgments, not your politically correct philosophy.

Ready, set, GO!

Money is:

1. _____

2. _____

3. _____

4. _____

5. _____

6. _____

7. _____

8. _____

9. _____

10. _____

What do you notice about your statements? Are there more positive or negative statements? Are they consistent or do some conflict with others? Do you recognize where some of these ideas may have come from? Let's go a step deeper.

What messages have you learned about money?

Write down all the messages you received about money while you were growing up. Was money talked about in your family, or was it a hidden subject? Did your parents argue about money? What did you learn about saving or generating money? How important was money among your friends? What attitudes did you learn about money from TV, the movies or church?

1. _____

2. _____

3. _____

4. _____

5. _____

6. _____

7. _____

8. _____

9. _____

10. _____

For some of you, money was never discussed openly in your family. Others may have been exposed to adult money concerns at too early an age. Money can be just as big a mystery in rich families as in poor ones. Many parents expect their children to know about money without teaching them about it, at least consciously. Unconsciously, our parents shape our attitudes about abundance by their words, behaviors, and even body language.

Money and Relationships

Perhaps one or both of your parents were so busy working for money, they didn't seem to have time for you. That can generate a polarization in your consciousness between love and money, a common theme in many movies and TV shows. Unfortunately, the internalized message becomes: you can have love, *or* you can have money, but you can't have both.

If your family constantly argued about money, even thinking about money is likely to trigger a lot of negative and confusing emotions. The belief you may have formed is, "Don't talk about it or someone's going to end up crying." At an early age, you may have associated money with uncomfortable emotions and decided to stop thinking about it. Consequently, you might not even know why you always seem to have problems with money.

When Susan landed her first big job, she was thrilled to phone her parents to share the great news. When her dad answered, Susan blurted out that soon she'd be earning a quarter-of-a-million dollars a year. There was no response, just silence. After a moment, it dawned on Susan that her father had never made a lot of money. It was obvious he was in conflict about hearing her news.

The conversation ended awkwardly and Susan hung up, feeling confused and vaguely guilty.

Subconsciously, the message Susan received was, "Making money interferes with my relationships, especially with men." Or, "If I make too much money, I'll lose love." In fact, Susan continued to earn lots of money, but she often had difficulty finding a partner who didn't feel threatened by her income until she consciously chose to release her subconscious guilt toward her father.

Money and Worth

Money is amazing stuff. It's absolutely useless unless it's being used in exchange for something. The dictionary definition of money is "a medium of exchange." But what are we exchanging it for? We might think we're buying a car or a pair of jeans, when we're really buying prestige. It's interesting to see what we exchange our money for. For some people, it's a good time, for others, it's things that make them feel better about themselves and for others still, it's an investment.

If you start to look at the money you spend, you'll realize that sometimes the return is only a moment's pleasure, and that's fine. Then there's the money you spend with no pleasure attached to it, like taxes. Sometimes you may feel like you're just throwing it away. I encourage you to think of your money as seeds you plant and grow, earning a return of some kind. Either you're planting your seeds in your own garden, or in someone else's.

What you gain isn't always monetary. For example, if you contribute to an organization that does good work in the world, you can watch that investment grow. While it's not actually making you money, it's creating something that you want to see increase.

What are some things you would do with a million dollars?

1. _____

2. _____

3. _____

4. _____

5. _____

6. _____

7. _____

8. _____

9. _____

10. _____

When you envision what purpose you will use money for, your vision creates a magnetic field that begins drawing money and other resources toward the realization of that goal.

The Power of Money

During a recent study, scientists measured the brain's response when a person looked at a pile of money. They were surprised to find that the mere sight of money initiates a chemical response as though the person had taken a drug. One suggested reason for this response is that money represents the potential of all possible pleasures. Paradoxically, it can also represent danger.

Several years ago, I changed banks and the format of the my new bank statement was different from what I was accustomed to. When I opened the envelope, at first glance, it looked like I had $100,000 more in the bank than I thought I had. Instantly, my heart started pounding and I felt a bit weak in the knees. Physiologically, my response was exactly the same as if I were to discover a large amount of money *missing* from my account. I was actually relieved to find the correct amount further down the statement.

It's obvious we have deep-seated, even physiological reactions, to the simple thought of lots of money. Rich people have lots of money. So let's explore what we think about them.

Rich people are...

We're going to do another free association exercise. This time, you'll write down your conceptions of rich people. Quickly write the first thing that comes to mind. It doesn't have to be consistent. I'm actually happier if it's not. Just see what comes up. Don't edit, just write. Think about Donald Trump. Think about Paris Hilton. Think about Oprah and Bill Gates. Ready, set, GO!

Rich people are:

1. _____

2. _____

3. _____

4. _____

5. _____

6. _____

7. _____

8. _____

9. _____

10. _____

Examine each of your answers. Which labels would you feel comfortable with for yourself? For instance, if you answered, "Rich people live in big houses" or "Rich people are politically influential," ask yourself "is that a good thing?" Or do you have a negative "charge" on that? Notice which of your attitudes toward wealthy people may be blocking your flow of abundance.

Poor people are...

Next, let's see what you feel about the poor. Ready, set, GO!

Poor people are:

1. _____

2. _____

3. _____

4. _____

5. _____

6. _____

7. _____

8. _____

9. _____

10. _____

What do you notice about your attitudes toward the poor? Do you hold the belief that your doing well will cause others to become or remain poor? What if you made so much money that you could do a lot of good in the world and help the poor? Can you see that your having an abundant life can enrich the lives of others, as well as your own?

Middle-class people are...

And we don't want to leave out the middle class. Ready, set, GO!

Middle-class people are:

1. _____

2. _____

3. _____

4. _____

5. _____

6. _____

7. _____

8. _____

9. _____

10. _____

One of the most common responses to this exercise is that middle-class people are *boring*. Sometimes it's more appealing to be a starving artist, musician or poet than to be financially comfortable. For those of us who are die-hard non-conformists, we want to avoid being seen as middle class and thus sentence ourselves to living marginally. Maybe we'll win the lottery one day or become an overnight sensation, but until then, we make sure people know that we couldn't care less about money.

As T. Harv Eker says, "If you say you don't care about money, I can tell you one thing for sure: You're broke!" Remember, abundance is a flow. It follows the path of least resistance. Don't resist money by affirming how little you care about it. If a friend told you repeatedly that they didn't care about you, would you want to hang around with them? It's the same with money.

What are your three biggest fears about money?

Simply state your three biggest fears about money.

1. _____

2. _____

3. _____

As you contemplate these fears, notice the emotions you are feeling and identify them as clearly as you can. What emotions besides fear are you experiencing? Anger? Sadness? Frustration? Hopelessness? Whatever the feelings are, acknowledge them and write them down below or on a separate sheet of paper.

_____

_____

_____

_____

_____

_____

_____

_____

Next, take a moment and scan your body with your awareness. What physical feelings do you notice? Don't try to change or fix anything, just collect the information. How does your head feel? Your throat? Your stomach? Your skin? What about your breathing? Again, make a few notes below or on a separate sheet of paper.

_____

_____

_____

_____

_____

Now, notice what thoughts are running through your head. What is The Little Voice saying? Write these thoughts below or on a separate sheet of paper.

_____

_____

_____

_____

_____

After you have written them down, restate them as a belief. For example, your thought may have been, *I don't have what it takes to succeed.* Write it in the form of a belief: "I believe I don't have what it takes to succeed."

_____

_____

_____

Acknowledge that you have discovered these beliefs and be glad you've identified the beliefs that have been driving your fears. Now you can choose whether to keep them or not. Think of those fearful thoughts as weeds in your inner garden. Pull out the weed and replace it with a healthy thought: "I have everything it takes to succeed!" Now write that down as your new affirmation.

_____

_____

_____

What do you love about money?

What do you love about money, or what would you love about money if you had more of it? Let your imagination soar. The sky is the limit. If necessary, use an extra sheet of paper to expand your vision of all the good things having a lot of money would bring into your life.

1. _____

2. _____

3. _____

4. _____

5. _____

6. _____

7. _____

8. _____

9. _____

10. _____

As in the previous exercise, take a moment to imagine yourself in your best-case scenario. What emotions come up for you? Make note of them, whether positive or negative.

1. _____

2. _____

3. _____

4.   _____

5.   _____

Now, turn your awareness toward your body and notice how
your body feels as you imagine all these good things. Write down
what you notice.

_____

_____

_____

_____

_____

Next, pay attention to the thoughts you're having as you
focus on your image of success and write those down.

_____

_____

_____

_____

_____

Answer the following question: Why don't or can't you have the life you just imagined? Write down the reasons.

_____

_____

_____

_____

_____

Restate each of these reasons as a belief.

_____

_____

_____

_____

_____

You now have the opportunity to choose which of those beliefs you want to grow in your garden and which are weeds. Pull out the weeds and be sure to replace them with new, positive statements. If you don't, the weeds will grow right back!

What new thoughts and feelings would you like to have about money and abundance?

Now that we know some of your existing beliefs about money, let's brainstorm ideas for new beliefs to replace them. Let's take the example of Susan's unhelpful beliefs:

She can change "If I make too much money, I'll lose love," to "I now have an abundance of love, money and all good things in my life." Susan's belief, "Making money interferes with my relationships, especially with men," can change to "Money enhances all my relationships."

1. _____

2. _____

3. _____

4. _____

5. _____

6. _____

7. _____

8. _____

9. _____

10. _____

Some Common Beliefs About Money

Let's say you have the belief that you have to work hard in order to earn money—a very common belief. It's repeated over and over, not just by family members, but by the media and popular culture. Let me ask you a question: Do you want to work hard for the rest of your life? Chances are, you answered no.

Already, we have a problem. If you're convinced that in order to make money, you have to work hard and you don't like working hard, what kind of results do you think you're going to get? Your belief will tend to keep you in a double-bind where you're either lacking money or you'll have money but resent working hard for it.

Ironically, most wealthy people will tell you that you can't become rich unless you learn how to generate passive income, where you're making money even while you sleep! In a way, the degree to which you believe you must work hard for your money is the degree to which you're blocking abundance. You can't possibly work enough hours and even if you could, you wouldn't have any free time to enjoy all that money you're making. One affirmation to apply to this belief is, "I make money awake or asleep, at work and or at play."

You want your beliefs to generate results you like. Your thoughts are creating reality, so you want to fill your subconscious with as many positive thoughts as possible. Like weeding, this is an ongoing process. There will always be a few weeds to manage in even the most beautiful garden. As you pull the weeds, you'll soon have many flowers blooming. And it gets easier as time goes on and the garden gets established.

Some of the thoughts you have about money and abundance may seem quite ridiculous once you look at them. However, some of your beliefs just need to be reframed. Reframing is a method used in hypnosis and neurolinguistic programming to see a situation in a different way.

For example, perhaps you have the belief that you need money to make money. If you don't have very much money, you may experience that belief as a limitation. If you look at people who have money and think, "They have money because they have money; I don't have money, so I don't have money," that's not a helpful point of view. However, you can reframe the belief to see every dollar as a seed, which you plant to make more money. In this case, it becomes a matter of learning the skill. And you can start with a single dollar. You can say, "It takes money to make money," in a positive way, feeling great about every dollar that comes your way because you recognize it as a money seed.

Sometimes people believe that money is for dessert. First you work hard for many years and then you retire. Only then can you relax and enjoy life. This belief says that you can't have fun and make money too. Work is work and fun is fun and never the twain shall meet. Remember the example of my mom and her resistance to going to Hawaii? Once she let go of the resistance, all the energy surrounding that belief disappeared. This cleared the way for the amazing possibility that she could book appointments while lounging by the pool. She actually made more money *because* she went away on vacation.

What if you loved getting up in the morning and going to work and not only got paid, but got paid a lot? What a concept! You have my permission to let go of the belief that you have to suffer to make money.

Another common belief is that you will have to sell out or change something about yourself to earn money. That's a belief you can change. In Southern California where I live, there's a popular affirmation that outrageously declares: "People pay me enormous sums of money for me being me." While there are lots of places in the world where that idea may seem impossible, in Hollywood it actually comes true. For example, Jack Black gets paid a lot of money simply for being who he is. Granted, who he is, is a lot of fun and he's extremely talented, but he doesn't put on any pretenses either. And leave it to Hollywood to create the idea of a "reality" show. It may be a low form of entertainment, but it's also an arena of possibility where people often get paid ridiculous amounts of money for simply being themselves, warts and all.

Chapter 9:
Self-Worth

Your relationship with money and abundance will often reflect your core beliefs about your worth. Some people believe they're simply not good enough, talented enough, smart enough, hard-working enough or educated enough to deserve wealth. To them, abundance only seems to be within the reach of fortunate, special people. When you unduly admire, envy or resent people just because they're wealthy, it's possible you are harboring the belief that you aren't worthy of having an abundant life.

You Are Worthy

At the heart of the abundance issue is a simple question: Are you willing to accept yourself as being perfectly okay, just as you are? When I attended The Money Seminar, one of the first things we were told was, "You are a child of the universe and you are loved." One of the women attending confessed, "I'm really having a hard time with the idea that I'm okay and that the universe loves me. I feel like I have to do all these things to earn love. And I'll never be perfect enough." How many of us are struggling with that belief?

Remember the two models of the universe: Scarcity and Abundance. Most of us were taught that there isn't enough of anything, including love. We've been taught that we must do certain things or be a certain way in order to earn love. That's the scarcity model.

Where does money come from? People! Where does love come from? People! Love, whether human or Divine, can only be expressed through the vehicle of a human being. When you realize that every human being is a potential fountain of love, you realize there is infinite love available, if only we would allow it to flow unconditionally. In the model of scarcity, people believe that somehow love will "run out." They withhold their love from themselves and others. Imagine a world where each person had a huge basket of delicious food, but they reluctantly shared it with others, and rarely put any of it in their own mouth. People are starving for love, even though it's abundantly available. This is the insanity of the scarcity model.

A New Story

What if you told yourself a new story about love? What if your new story said you were loveable just as you are? How would that new story change your life? What if that story were true for everyone on earth? The universe created you to experience life, a great gift. Life is amazingly strong. Life is abundance. You have a right—a birthright—to participate in the flow. No one can take that away.

Too Good for Money

On the opposite side of the coin, we find people who believe that money is beneath them. They may feel they're too good, too pure or too spiritual to be concerned with money. This category often includes artists and musicians, or healers who are conflicted about accepting money for their services. If you understand that money is simply energy, perhaps you'll agree that it's perfectly fine for you to be supported energetically. Remember that money is a symbol of human energy. It's simply a medium of exchange. The only value and meaning it has is what you decide to give it.

Guilt About Money

There are also those who feel guilty about money. They believe it wouldn't be fair for them to prosper, as long as there are others who are in poverty. As Wayne Dyer points out, your feeling bad or guilty has never helped another human being. You can't heal anyone by feeling bad and you can't feed anyone with your guilt. However, if you were to allow abundance to flow into your life, you would have the power to do a lot of good for your fellow man.

Fear of Making Mistakes

Albert Einstein said, "Anyone who has never made a mistake has never tried anything new." To him, mistakes were learning opportunities. You'll find that people in all walks of life who are successful, make a lot of mistakes and they learn from them. They use mistakes as stepping stones to what does work.

Most of us raised our hands in second grade, made a mistake, got shamed for it and became stuck there. We may be operating in the world with a second grader's fear of being wrong and getting a bad mark next to our name. This keeps us closed-in and small, which slows down the flow of energy and abundance. When we're afraid to make mistakes, we don't allow ourselves the freedom to find out what's possible.

> *When I told my friends I was going to be a comedian,*
> *they laughed at me.*
>
> —Carrot Top

In terms of finding out what's possible and what's not, it's good to go out there and mix it up a bit. Try some things on for size. Start with some of the ideas in this book. Do you want to stay safe and small or are you willing to risk making a mistake? Do you believe you are a failure, because you tried something once and it didn't work out? Successful people are powerful in the face of "no." In order to do that, you have to get comfortable with making mistakes and maybe even doing it publicly. I'm not saying that making a mistake is fun, though it can be. If you begin to affirm that mistakes are simply information or feedback, it makes things much easier. Sometimes "wrong" is just the sensation you feel when you let go of a dearly held belief.

> *I'm not a genius, I've just made a lot more mistakes*
> *than most people.*
>
> —Buckminster Fuller

Chapter 10:
Integrity

Aligning Thought, Word and Deed

Integrity helps to create great results fast. My definition of integrity is when everything about you—your thoughts, words and actions, and your conscious, subconscious and soul—are one and aligned. When that happens, you become unstoppable.

If your conscious intention and your subconscious beliefs are out of alignment, failure is almost guaranteed. A power struggle will be going on inside that will sabotage your efforts to move forward toward your goals. If you'd like to change something in your life, it's a good idea to include the subconscious in your plans.

Think of it this way: If your conscious mind had all the answers, you wouldn't be having the problem. If the conscious mind were totally in control, everything would be perfect. Someone once said, in a battle between the conscious and the unconscious, the unconscious always wins.

When you perceive that something is keeping you from experiencing what you want to experience in life, you might identify some external factors and some as internal. However, the degree to which you can change the world around you depends on the degree to which you can master the world inside you.

Throughout this book, we've been examining our thoughts about abundance, whether conscious, subconscious or automatic. You may have discovered that many of your beliefs don't support your goals. When your thoughts don't support your goals, your actions don't either. As a consequence, you don't get the results you want. The trick is to notice when your thoughts aren't helpful and plant new, positive thoughts.

Weeding Your Garden

The metaphor I keep returning to is the garden. Every garden has weeds. If you only pull the weeds and don't plant anything else, then the weeds grow back. But if you pull the weeds and plant flowers in their place, soon the flowers become the dominant plants in the garden. Yes, there will still be weeds at times, but your garden will be easier to maintain.

In the beginning, you may discover a lot of weeds, but remember that the key to subconscious learning is repetition. Don't be afraid of your thoughts. You want them to poke their little heads out so you can keep your garden weeded. Then you have the opportunity of turning them around so that you can have a new, positive statement to plant in your subconscious.

This is where affirmations and guided visualizations can be powerful allies. By focusing and training your subconscious with a new thought, you begin to create new actions, new results and a new reality. By changing your thoughts by a tiny degree at the beginning, you can end up in a completely different destination.

For example, if money and hard work are tied together in your mind, pull out that weed and plant the affirmation, "I make money at work and at play. I relax, do my best and the world is wonderful." If you believe it's hard to make a living, plant a new thought in its place. Say to yourself, "I make plenty of money doing work I love."

If you don't have money or are in debt, focus on the thought, "I have all the money I need," or, "My income now far exceeds my expenses." Remind yourself that what you focus on increases. Focus your conscious mind on what you want to create, rather than on your problem. And use affirmations and visualizations to begin bringing the subconscious into alignment with your conscious intention.

At first, you may feel an inner resistance to some of the affirmations, because you may have overdeveloped negative "mental muscles." Keep practicing the exercises in the next chapter and soon your positive mental muscles will grow even stronger. Chances are, you've been practicing one way of thinking for most of your life. Experts say it takes twenty-one days to form a new habit. See what happens when you practice a different way of thinking for the next three weeks.

Remember the epiphany at the beginning of the book: consciousness is evolving. We're all learning this. It's not something you do once and never do again. Integrity is a way of being in the world that needs to be exercised and developed. Integrity is a habit, like brushing your teeth or going to the gym.

Tell No Lies

In *The Millionaire Mind*, Thomas J. Stanley interviewed many self-made millionaires to find out what they thought had contributed most to their success. It turned out that intelligence and education were rather far down the list. Want to guess the number one factor?

You may be surprised to learn that the number one factor self-made millionaires identified as most important to their success was, "Being honest with all people."

According to Stanley's research, millionaires tend to have very high values, especially around truth-telling. When you tell the truth, your thoughts, words and actions are in alignment. Whenever you are tempted to be less than honest, you are living within the scarcity model of the universe. If you want to create a new abundant reality, it will happen faster if you are congruent in thought, word and deed.

Integrity is the essence of everything successful.
—Buckminster Fuller

Keeping Your Word

Integrity also means honoring your Word. As you discovered in the chapter on The Power of Your Word, the words you say are important. This is especially true if you make a promise. There is a lot of power in saying what you will do and then doing what you said. Every time you do so, you're putting the universe on notice that you are a person who is consciously creating reality with your Word.

If you make a promise, do your level best to keep it. If for some reason you can't, restore your integrity as soon as possible by communicating with the person and simply apologizing. It may sound strange, but it's sometimes better not to make excuses, even if you have a really good one. This is because an excuse is often a negative belief in disguise. You don't want to reinforce it by letting that belief get you off the hook! Of course, an explanation may be necessary, just don't turn that explanation into an excuse. You, and only you, will be able to tell the difference.

A lot of trouble in this world could be avoided if people never said yes when they really meant no. Social conditioning has us well trained. If someone asks you for a favor, you are very likely to say okay, unless you have a good reason why you can't. Cheryl Richardson describes this as saying yes because you don't have an "absolute no." If you're a person who never has time for yourself, Cheryl suggests you practice saying no, unless you feel an absolute inner "yes!" What a concept! Imagine how your life would change if your days were filled with activities and projects that made your body, mind and soul say "Yes!" That would be true integrity.

Passion: Loving What You Do

Enthusiasm and love are two things that really help the garden of abundance grow. So what do you love to do? What if the people, things and activities you loved were the top priorities in your life? When you wake up in the morning, you want the feeling that you're thrilled to be alive. If you believe that when you do what you love, you will be sustained by the universe financially and energetically, you'll be well on your way to creating that reality.

Twenty Things You Love To Do

What are twenty things you love to do or would love to do if you could do anything?

1. _____

2. _____

3. _____

4. _____

5. _____

6. _____

7. _____

8. _____

9. _____

10. _____

11. _____

12. _____

13. _____

14. _____

15. _____

16. _____

17. _____

18. _____

19. _____

20. _____

Once you have twenty items listed, prioritize them. Here's how to do it quickly. Take the first two items, decide which you love more and write it down. Then take the next two items, decide which of those you love more and write that down. Continue through your list of twenty items until you've narrowed it down to the ten items you love most. Then repeat the until you've identified the one thing you love to do most.

Now, imagine about how you can make money doing that thing:

1. _____

2. _____

3. _____

4. _____

5. _____

This isn't as far-fetched as it might sound. Let's say that you love sleeping above everything else. How can you make money in your sleep? Here are five ways: interest on investments, royalties, real estate income, real estate appreciation and online sales. You could even be a paid subject is a sleep research lab. If you started this book with the idea that you have to work hard to make money, you now have good evidence that you can sleep and make money at the same time!

If you could do anything, knowing you could not fail, list five things you would do.

1. _____

2. _____

3. _____

4. _____

5. _____

What is stopping you?

1. _____

2. _____

3. _____

4. _____

5. _____

What beliefs do you notice behind the reasons stopping you? Write the above reasons in the form of beliefs and see if there are any you want to affirm.

1. _____

2. _____

3. _____

4. _____

5. _____

For example, you may have said, "I can't because I'm too old." Restated as a belief instead of "reality," the statement changes to "I believe I can't because I'm too old." Now it's up to you to determine if that belief is really true. If your dream is to be an Olympic Gold Medallist and you're sixty years old, well perhaps it's true, although I know of several Ironman

Triathletes who are sixty and older. In 2001, at age seventy-seven, Bill Bell was the oldest official Ironman Triathalon finisher in sixteen hours, fifty-seven minutes and sixteen seconds. If you believe you're "too old" to learn to dance, or to be an actor, or to write a novel, you may want to transform that belief.

Affirmations and goal setting are powerful tools for transforming beliefs. That is what the next chapter will teach you how to do.

Chapter 11:
Changework: Affirmations
and Goal Setting

People are not lazy. They simply have impotent goals—
that is, goals that do not inspire them.

—Anthony Robbins

Jim Carrey

When Jim Carrey was still a struggling actor working in comedy clubs, he used to drive up to the top of Mulholland Drive to look out over the city of Los Angeles and visualize his success. To make his reality even more solid, he wrote a check in the amount of ten million dollars to "Jim Carrey for acting services rendered," dating it Thanksgiving Day, 1995. He carried that check with him for years.

By the time 1995 came, Jim Carrey had made *Ace Ventura, The Mask, Dumb & Dumber* and *Batman Forever*. Not only could he have cashed that check, he could have cashed it several times over. Jim Carrey set that goal very purposefully. Others set their goals quite naturally.

Sarah Hughes

Sarah Hughes won the Olympic gold in figure skating in 2002 in Salt Lake City. She was sixteen years old and a surprise winner. When she won, the television networks played a video of Sarah when she was just six years old. She'd won a local figure skating competition and a reporter asked her, "What do you want to be when you grow up?" Sarah replied, "When I grow up, I'm going to go to the Olympics and win a gold medal. I can hardly wait!"

I believe there was a direct connection between that moment of declaration and her subsequent victory at the Olympics. In that moment, Sarah didn't have an inkling of doubt. She didn't know she "couldn't," so she planted the seed with her affirmation. Not only did she say she'd do it, she had an "I can't wait!" attitude. Sarah had to do a lot of practice along the way, but it was only natural that she would win a gold medal in the Olympics ten years later.

Perhaps The Little Voice in your head is reminding you of all those Olympic hopefuls who had similar thoughts and didn't win gold medals. While there's a chance you may not reach your goals even if you affirm them, it's even truer that you're very unlikely to reach them if you don't believe you can. Remember Henry Ford's claim about people who think they can and people who think they can't: they're both right!

Buckminster Fuller

In 1927, at the age of thirty-two, Buckminster Fuller decided to throw himself into the icy waters of Lake Michigan. He was bankrupt and unemployed and his child had died. In the depths of depression, he heard a small voice say, "You do not have the right to end your life. It is not yours to end. Your life has a purpose. You have not yet done what you came here to do."

This was a turning point for Buckminster Fuller. He decided to recreate himself from scratch and live his life as "an experiment, to find what a single individual can contribute to changing the world and benefiting all humanity."

A lot of wonderful things came from that decision, including twenty-five US patents, twenty-eight books and dozens of major architectural designs. He's most famous as the creator of the geodesic dome, which is a physical manifestation of tensegrity: the principle that if you put pressure on something, it doesn't get weaker, but stronger. Geodesic domes are incredibly stable structures—they get stronger if you heap weight on them and they can't fall down in an earthquake—yet they use less material to span a larger unobstructed space than any other structure.

Buckminster Fuller's use of resources was incredibly efficient. He was one of the earliest proponents of renewable energy, maintaining that "there is no energy crisis, only a crisis of ignorance." During his long and productive life, Fuller circled the globe over fifty times, teaching millions through his books, public lectures and interviews.

Most of us have lesser goals. Buckminster Fuller's goal was to find out how much he could personally contribute to the world. What contributions could you make to humanity? When you have a big goal like that, you increase the flow of energy and abundance not only into your life, but also into the lives of others. That's the power of a big goal.

Working With Affirmations

One of the most powerful tools you can use to shift your reality is affirmations. Affirmations are statements you repeat to yourself in order to program your subconscious mind with positive new thoughts. The more often they are repeated, the sooner you will be creating your new reality. Think, say and write your affirmations. Print them on cards and place them where you can see them throughout the day.

Affirmations can also help pave the way to achieving your more audacious goals. Before Mark Victor Hansen and Robert G. Allen began writing their marvelous book, *The One Minute Millionaire: The Enlightened Way to Wealth,* they created a mock-up of a *Publishers' Weekly* front-page story, dated one year in the future, announcing their new book had broken all records for first-day sales. A year later, nearly to the day, the book almost did break Amazon's record for first-day sales, second only to one of the Harry Potter books. Not only *Publishers' Weekly*, but also *The New York Times* carried cover stories about their success.

In Appendix A of this book, there's a list of affirmations for abundance. Later in this chapter, I'll also teach you how to create your own affirmations.

Start an Affirmation Journal

I encourage you to repeat your affirmations in writing, at least in the beginning. The written word brings thought into physical manifestation. Once written, it physically exists on a piece of paper. I suggest you hand write your affirmations, rather than typing them. Handwriting has more of your energy in it; it's more tactile and therefore kinetically felt.

I also suggest you begin keeping an affirmation journal.Don't make it fancy; a spiral bound notebook is fine. It's not writing you're going to keep. It's about the process.

Practice

Practice using the following written affirmation: "I, (insert your first name), deserve to be healthy, wealthy and prosperous."

Including your name in the affirmation helps you feel more powerfully connected to health, wealth and prosperity. Write the affirmation in your notebook and notice how it feels. Do you believe it? Continue writing the affirmation several times in a row, say five to ten times. Notice how you feel when you've finished.

Keep track of your feelings and thoughts as you write

Sometimes when we write a new affirmation, we stir up some objections. I like to make note of those objections, because they give me a hint at a core belief I may not be consciously aware of.

It's a good idea to notice what The Little Voice is saying at this point, because it will reveal where you may need to do some deeper work.

For example, perhaps you have the thought, *Who do you think you are?* or *That's a crock!* as you write the affirmation. Perhaps you have a self-esteem problem or a belief that you have to be a certain way or be someone special in order to deserve anything good at all. Those thoughts reveal exactly where you're stuck. You can then create a new affirmation to deal with whatever objections The Little Voice raises, such as: "I deserve to be happy and prosperous whether or not I am perfect." You get the idea.

Continue writing the affirmation in the first person until it feels believable. This may only take a few minutes for some affirmations, for others, several days. The important thing is to continue writing each affirmation five to ten times daily until it feels natural when you say it.

Write the affirmation in the second and third person

Next, write the affirmation in the second person: "You, (insert your first name), deserve to be healthy, wealthy and prosperous." This helps to re-pattern the messages you heard from your parents, authority figures and peers. Write this affirmation five to ten times daily until it feels real.

Finally, write your affirmation in the third person: "He or She, (insert your first name), deserves to be healthy, wealthy and prosperous." This lets you experience the sense of others seeing you in your new reality.

Personally, I find the third-person affirmations about abundance are often the most challenging, because I tend to hold a core belief that others may resent me if I'm successful. Many people have a similar unconscious belief. Maybe because we know we've resented other people's success we fear our own success will be resented too.

When I was working with this affirmation, I had to admit my own attitudes toward the wealthy were often less than kind. However, noticing this was enough for me to begin shifting my thoughts. What if I began holding positive thoughts toward wealthy and prosperous people? What if I celebrated their prosperity, rather than being jealous or feeling threatened? What if I let go of my pet assumptions that rich people were oblivious to other people's suffering, that they were even the cause of other people's suffering? I began to use a different lens on my filter to look for examples of great philanthropy among the wealthy. I remembered the Golden Rule; do unto others. I affirmed, "I bless and celebrate others' abundance."

It's powerful to experience the impact of your affirmation from these three perspectives. Any parts of you that aren't in alignment will quickly show up. The Little Voice will say, "Um, I don't think so," or, "Remember that time when you failed?" or "What if I make a mistake?" When fear of making mistakes holds you back, remind yourself of what Buckminster Fuller said: "The degree to which I succeed is the degree to which I'm willing to make mistakes." Take those negatives and put them into a positive statement.

As you reprogram your subconscious, your filters will begin to draw your attention to all those things in the environment that are going to help bring your new reality into being. Repeating the affirmation so it becomes automatic will help immensely.

Affirmations and Healing

As you may have noticed, working with affirmations can uncover hidden aspects of yourself that are calling for healing. As I worked with affirmations about increasing my wealth, I began to experience a feeling of fear growing deep in my belly. It's not easy to share this, but it was such a profound realization, I feel I must.

At that time, I was in my mid-twenties and newly married. For the first time, I felt like my own person, with a newfound identity, independent of my family. I was feeling really good about finding my own way. Until the moment I felt that uncomfortable feeling in my stomach, I had no idea I had a secret fear. As I contemplated the fearful feeling, I suddenly realized I held a belief that if I had a lot of money, all my relatives would want to move in with me and I'd be stuck with them forever. My family might become dependent on me, just as I was beginning to enjoy my own freedom in life. If they needed me to support them financially, I would be too uncomfortable to say no. As far as my subconscious was concerned, the easiest solution was to avoid the whole problem by only allowing my money situation to improve a little, but not too much.

Now, I'd never thought about this consciously, but on a deep level, this core belief was like a valve controlling the amount of abundance I was willing to allow into my life. I realized I had a picture of my mother and two sisters as financially needy and unable to take care of themselves in the world. My next step was to create the affirmation, "My sisters and mother have everything they need to prosper. They deserve to be healthy, wealthy and prosperous too." I didn't want anything in my imagination to hold them in a place of dependency.

To my surprise, writing those words uncovered an even deeper core issue. Part of the reason I felt I deserved to be wealthy and prosperous was because I thought I *did* deserve it. I'd always been very responsible, an excellent student, even a bit of a perfectionist. I'd worked hard to do all the "right" things. I deserved to be doing well in life. I was the only one in my family who had managed to get a college education and I'd paid my own way with scholarships and part-time jobs. What if they received all these things too, without doing any of the work?

It was hard to face, but I suddenly realized that I secretly felt a bit superior to them. I was in a double-bind. I had an investment in them achieving less than I did and at the same time I was afraid to make very much money because I feared I would have to support them. I could see these fears were keeping me from opening the doors to abundance. It was uncomfortable to recognize, but it was also liberating to bring these feelings into full consciousness. In twenty minutes of writing affirmations, I worked through an issue that might have taken years of traditional therapy to resolve.

I weeded my inner garden and planted new seeds: "I deserve to be wealthy and prosperous, they deserve to be wealthy and prosperous, everyone deserves to be wealthy and prosperous." As I released the need to feel "special" or "better than," my fear of having money subsided.

Fear of Success

Unconsciously, many of us are as afraid of success as we are of failure. We may fear that our success will make someone we love feel inferior. Perhaps there is a fear of standing out in a crowd, of being seen. We may worry about incurring the resentment and jealousy of other people. Such hidden fears may be grounded in past experience. Or they may be somewhat irrational, as in my secret belief: "If I have money, my family will move in with me and I'll never be able to have my own private life or have children." Through affirmations, I became aware of my fears and released them, which helped tremendously.

Real confidence comes not from ignoring your fears.
Rather, it comes from learning what those fears have to teach,
and then moving ahead more fully prepared.
—Ralph Marston

The Anatomy of a Good Affirmation

Affirmations are a powerful tool to discover and transform many core beliefs that are standing in your way. What follows is a guide to creating your own positive affirmations.

A good affirmation is a message to your subconscious mind. In order to work effectively, it must use the kind of language your subconscious mind can easily understand. Remember that your sub-conscious mind is very literal. It tends to hear what you are actually saying, not what you may think you are saying. Here are some rules for creating affirmations that work.

1. Positive

Be sure to start with a positive statement. Remember you want to focus on the reality you want to manifest, so don't focus on the problem. The best affirmations aren't about fixing or changing the "old" reality. They redirect your focus, and therefore your energy, toward the new reality you wish to create.

Don't say: "I am going to lose twenty pounds."

Do say: "My body perfectly balances my intake of food with healthy activity," or "I now eat just the right amount to maintain the perfect healthy weight for me."

Remember that your subconscious mind is literal. Saying "I need to," or "I want to," tends to keep you within the reality of *needing* and *wanting* rather than in the reality of *having*.

Restate the following sentences in positive terms:

"I am no longer in pain."

"I need a new car."

"I want to make lots and lots of money, but not at a job I don't like."

"I release from my life all the things I hate."

2. Present Tense

Make sure your affirmations are always stated in the present tense. If you say to your subconscious mind, "I am going to..." it hears "someday," as in "someday I am going to." Someday never comes. Make the statement about now, not a vague future time.

Don't say: "I am going to be a successful author."

Do say: "I am now becoming a successful author."

Or more simply: "I am now a successful author."

3. Personal

Your subconscious has been trained to pay attention to the sound of your name, therefore it can be very powerful to include at least your first name in your affirmation.

"I, Linda, am now a very successful author."

See what I mean? It helps you own your power.

It's also a good exercise to write or state your affirmations in the second and third person, again with your first name. It may be one thing for you to make an affirmation privately, but what if others are saying it about you too? You may be surprised at your reaction to hearing the words as though they're being said *to* you or *about* you instead of by you.

"I, Luke, deserve to be wealthy, prosperous and happy."

"You, Luke, deserve to be wealthy, prosperous and happy."

"He, Luke, deserves to be wealthy, prosperous and happy."

4. Authentic

Your Spirit loves truth. It's important that your affirmations feel true for you. Notice I said *true*, not *realistic*. There's a big difference. By the way, your definition of *realistic* will certainly expand as you work with affirmations. However, to begin by stating, "I am a millionaire," may not feel true *enough*, at first, to engage your Spirit. Also, it bears repeating that abundance is more about flow, than accumulation. However, saying, "I deserve to be wealthy, happy and prosperous," is an innate truth your Spirit can and will connect with. Your Spirit agrees that you truly do deserve to be wealthy, happy and prosperous, even if your mind doesn't yet believe it.

At the same time, it's a good exercise to challenge and even stretch your current notions of reality. Here's a little secret you may want to try. The next time you "have to" do something you don't usually enjoy doing, try restating the task with the words "get to." Try it!

Say, "I have to do the dishes." Now say, "I *get* to do the dishes!" Your subconscious will hear a very different message and you may find doing the dishes more pleasant, even enjoyable. At least, you'll probably laugh.

Years ago, I tried this experiment with something none of us really likes.

"I get to pay my taxes!" I was standing in line at the Kealakekua post office waiting to mail my quarterly income tax deposit to the government. Instead of complaining, I started playing with the thought, "I get to pay my taxes!" At first it seemed to be a ridiculous statement, then suddenly I realized that most of the folks in line with me that afternoon were among the most prosperous in our small town. We all "got to" pay our quarterly taxes because we were business owners and we were making money! From that moment on, I began to think of paying taxes as a symbol of prosperity. I affirm the universe is abundant; there is always plenty for me, with or without taxes.

Don't say: "I have to drive the kids to school."

Do say: "I get to drive the kids to school. Lucky me!"

5. Clear

Make your affirmations clear and concise, using simple language even a child could understand. Since many of your core beliefs were formed when you were a child, you want to be sure the youngest part of you understands your new instructions. K.I.S.S., Keep it simple, sweetheart!

Don't say: "I now am incubating positive and evolved opinions of myself even when I haven't fulfilled or completed my own or other peoples' expectations, in my relationships with other individuals or groups."

Do say: "I love and accept myself exactly as I am."

Or: "I like me!"

6. Energetic

Remember that beliefs form within your subconscious through intensity as well as through repetition. Energy commands attention and attention directs energy. Choosing words that hold maximum energy for you, increases the power of your intention or as Tony Robbins might say, will *massively* increase the power.

Don't say: "I have just enough money to cover my rent."

Do say: "People give me *enormous* amounts of money for work I *love* doing!"

Also consider the quality of energy you wish to create in your life. Do you want to be highly energized and active, or would you like to become relaxed and easy going? Either way, you may want to consider adding positive descriptive words to your statements, such as "easy and effortless," "joyful," "healthy" and "fun."

You can say: "Day by day I am learning and growing."

It's better to say: "I explore my full human potential with joy and courage!"

7. For the Highest Good of All

Over the years, people who work with affirmations have developed phrases that help insure that what they are affirming will manifest in the most integrated and positive way. My favorite tag lines to add to almost any affirmation are the following:

"This or something better, for the highest good of all."

And this one I learned from Marc Allen's wonderful book, *The Millionaire Course*:

"In an easy and relaxed manner, in healthy and positive ways, in perfect timing for my highest good and the highest good of all."

A note about perfect timing: Sometimes perfect timing isn't what we envisioned. My affirmation, "I am always in the right place at the right time," is great for moving easily through traffic. On the way to work I usually get a lot of green lights. However, the other morning I seemed to hit every light just as it turned red. I was still going to be on time, but it would be close. Just as I began to get frustrated, I came across the scene of a serious three-car accident that had happened minutes before. Perhaps those red lights helped me be in the right place at the right time after all. I immediately thanked my traffic signal angels for keeping me out of harm's way.

Treasure Maps

Treasure maps are visual affirmations. Collect clippings from magazines and brochures of things you would like to manifest in your life. The images can be literal depictions or they can be symbolic. You can also collect words or phrases that inspire you, including a few of your favorite affirmations. Create a collage of your ideal scenes and words. This is your treasure map.

Put your treasure map on your refrigerator or somewhere where you can see it every day. You can also make mini-treasure maps in your journal. Continue to add things to your treasure map to reflect your goals or create a separate treasure map for a new goal or project. It's uncanny how many of them will come true.

My friends Sue and Dennis took a photograph of themselves kayaking in front of a waterfront home they really liked. They put the photo up on their refrigerator and affirmed they would soon have that house or something better. Within a year, they found and purchased the same model house, only with a slightly better floor plan.

Sharon created a treasure map in which she made visible her intention to take all her grandchildren to Disneyland. She pasted photos of herself and each of her grandchildren next to a picture of the Magic Kingdom. By the end of that year, she had fulfilled her promise. A few years later, she had the fantasy of buying a Range Rover and driving it across the country. It was an expensive car, a little out of her budget. She thought, *What the heck, I'll put it on my treasure map*. Within a short time, she found a Range Rover at a great price. She bought it and had a wonderful time driving all over the US.

What You Focus on Increases

> *Obstacles are those frightening things that become*
> *visible when we take our eyes off our goals.*
>
> —Henry Ford

There is a metaphysical law that says what you focus on increases. This is why it is so important not to focus on your problems. Don't even focus on the solution. Simply focus on the reality you would like to create.

Luke was vacationing in Maui when he impulsively decided to join a bicycle ride down the slopes of Haleakala, the dormant volcano in the center of the island. He didn't want to miss this rare opportunity, and even though he hadn't ridden a bike in years, he signed up at once.

The route was almost entirely downhill, with hundreds of sharp bends. With oncoming cars speeding past on his left, and low or nonexistent guardrails protecting him from careening down the mountain on his right, he started to become nervous at every bend in the road. As Luke awkwardly negotiated each turn, he kept his hands squeezing hard on the brakes and his eyes fixed on the sharp drop-off at the edge of the road.

Then Luke remembered what he'd learned in a motorcycle training course: Your bike goes where you look. *Don't look at the obstacle. Look at where you want to go.*

As hard as it was for him to ignore a drop-off he was rapidly approaching, he turned his head to look at the road where the turn ended. On some hairpin turns, this meant Luke was actually looking over his shoulder. Almost as if by magic, the bike started to turn on its own. He didn't have to think about the handlebars or worry about the road immediately in front of him.

Using this technique of simply looking toward the end of difficult turns, focusing on his goal, Luke was able to complete the ride safely, successfully and with immense pleasure.

Four Leaf Clovers and Sharks' Teeth

My mother has always been lucky at finding four leaf clovers, but it had been a while since she'd tried to find one. Just for fun, she decided to start looking for them whenever she walked her dog. Within three weeks, she had found thirty-seven. One of those days, she found fifteen during a twenty-minute walk through the park near her apartment. I saw them with my own eyes. This morning she called me to report she'd just found a five leaf clover. "There was a four leaf clover too. I didn't see it until I picked the one with five leaves, because it was very tiny."

My friend Judi has a similar talent for finding fossilized sharks' teeth. She's an amazing beachcomber with a stupendous collection of seashells she's found on her morning strolls along the beach on Hilton Head Island. Fossilized sharks' teeth in that part of the world are very tiny, usually no more than half an inch long. They're black and shiny, easily mistaken for broken pieces of mussel shell, which are scattered on the sand in great number. For three months I combed the very same beach looking for my very own shark's tooth, but to no avail. Sometimes I'd walk with Judi, both of us searching for the tiny treasures. I would find none, but Judi would always find at least three or four to add to her collection, which now fills several large mayonnaise jars.

One day as I was walking on the beach with Judi, she said, "Linda, let me draw you a circle so you can find one." It felt like cheating, but I'd been searching in vain all afternoon so I said okay. She reached down and drew a perfect twelve-inch circle in the wet sand right at my feet. I blinked to make sure. There, glistening in the center of the circle was a tiny, perfectly formed fossilized shark's tooth. "I was worried you were going to step on it!" Judi said, winking at me and smiling.

"How do you do it, Judi?"

"Oh, it's easy!" she said. She has the mayonnaise jars to prove it.

In case you were wondering, it isn't just me. None of Judi's neighbors find many sharks' teeth either. Judi is the champion. While the rest of us walk the beach muttering how sharks' teeth are next to impossible to find, Judi affirms that it's easy.

And that makes all the difference.

COUPON EXPIRES:
December 31, 2006

2700168

SAVE 50¢

Valid on all 900ml ARTHUR'S fresh juices and smoothies

www.arthursjuice.com

Appendix A: Affirmations for Abundance

The universe is abundant; there is plenty for all.

I deserve to be prosperous, healthy and happy!

I am a generous giver and an excellent receiver.

Good things are coming my way.

I am always in exactly the right place at the right time.

I bless and celebrate others' prosperity as I bless and celebrate my own.

Abundance is now flowing freely into my life.

I now have more than enough money for all my needs and heart's desires.

The money I spend comes back to me multiplied.

→ I now have a satisfying income of more than $_____ per month.

I make money whether I am awake or asleep, at work or at play.

I make lots of money doing work that I love.

Every day I am growing more financially prosperous and free.

→ I am willing to be happy and successful.

I now release guilt, fears and self-blame.

I am financially successful whether I work hard or not.

My negative self-images are now dissolving; I relax, do my best and the world is beautiful.

I love and appreciate myself.

People honor and value my work and they tell me so.

I give thanks for all the good things that are coming into my life.

I am open to receive all the good the universe wants to gift me.

I acknowledge and express my good, which is flowing through me at all times.

The more I receive, the more good I can do in the world.

Money is a symbol of human energy; as long as there are plenty of people, there is plenty of money.

My income now far exceeds my expenses.

Appendix B: Guided Visualization for Abundance

A form of self-hypnosis, guided visualization is a kind of highly focused daydreaming. Good guided visualization reprograms your subconscious mind by focusing your attention, your intention, your will and your imagination on the goals you wish to manifest. It's also deeply relaxing, helping you to relax and renew your mind, body and spirit.

I suggest you tape yourself reading the following script. As you read the words, say them slowly, using your voice to accentuate the words that appear in italicized type. Pause for a few seconds at the places indicated by an ellipse (…). Be sure to pause for a full ten seconds between each paragraph to give yourself time to develop the imagery as you listen.

You may also order pre-recorded tapes or CDs from www.lindagabriel.com.

I suggest you listen to your tape once a day for two to three weeks, then whenever you feel the need thereafter. Listen to your tape any time you want to take a relaxing break, but **never in the car** or any time you need to consciously focus on a task.

Many people listen as they're going to sleep at night and that's fine. Don't worry if you fall asleep before the end of the tape, because your subconscious will hear every word. If you decide to listen only at night, consider using the alternate ending, which suggests you will sleep deeply and peacefully until morning.

Begin recording and remember to speak slowly.

Begin by getting into a comfortable position, either lying down or sitting down…

Take a moment to adjust your body, making sure your head and neck are comfortably supported… And then… when you are as *comfortable* as can be… you may begin… by allowing…

several... slow... deep... *relaxing* breaths... *Inhaling* through your nose... and *exhaling* through your nose or mouth, whichever feels more comfortable...

And as you breathe in... you want to be sure... to inhale *deeply*... all the way into the belly... so that... with each *deep* inhalation... you can *feel* the belly gently expand... and with each slow, *complete* exhalation... feel the belly gently *relax*... And you want to be *sure*... to take several... slow... deep... *relaxing* breaths... before you begin... to breathe normally.

Imagine... breathing in... feelings of *comfort*... feelings of *safety*...feelings of calm... peaceful... quiet... *relaxation*...

And as you breathe out... you can imagine... breathing out... any and all *tension*... Breathing out... any and all *discomfort*... breathing out any and all *tightness*... Letting go... of problems and worries... Letting go and *relaxing*... even deeper... and *deeper* still... with each more... *relaxing*... breath.

Now... begin to imagine... a beautiful, safe place in Nature... perhaps a place you have been before... or you may just create it within yourself...

This is your own *private* sanctuary... A place where you can go anytime you need to... or wish to... Nothing and no one can harm you here... Notice how *beautiful* and *peaceful* it is... and how *good* it feels to be there... Notice the beauty of the landscape... the colors...the sounds... there may even be... a *wonderful* scent in the air... it's all up to *you*...

This is a place where... you can connect with... your *deepest* wisdom... and *highest* guidance... A safe place... A *healing* space... A *sacred* place within...

If you haven't already... find a place in your sanctuary... where you may rest... *comfortably*... sitting down... or lying down...

Notice the *breeze* stirring the *leaves*... on the trees... Perhaps a few clouds... drifting gently... across the sky... and a bright *light*... shining down... between the clouds... reaching you... and helping you... to relax... even *deeper*...

And this *light*... stands for all things *good* in life... such as... *Abundance*... *Peace*... *Joy*... Unconditional *Love*... *Happiness*... *Success*... *Tranquility* and vibrant *Health*...

Allow this light to begin flowing through you *now*... from your head... on out through your fingers... and toes... Bathing your *entire* being in *light*... your energy field... your physical body... your *brain*... rinsing away... any remaining tension or tightness... which may have been stored in the body... All guilt... self-blame and resentment are released... *NOW*... The light *heals* and *balances* every tissue... every cell... *healing* and *restoring*... every part of you... *clearing away* old ideas... beliefs... *emotions*... thoughts... memories... that no longer... serve your highest good... bringing you into more perfect *harmony*... with yourself... and your world.

Deep within... at *every* level of your mind... and *soul*... at the *core*... of your being... you are *aware*... that the universe... is *safe*. There is abundance for *all*... There is *always*... more than enough... for every single soul... on this planet... including *you*... and that each one of us... *including* you... *deserve*... to live... a healthy... loving... happy... *abundant* life...

You have opened an inner door... Step into the *glowing*... *flowing*... sunlight... of *abundance*... in all of its *wonderful*... manifestations... Abundance is *satisfying*... *creative*... work... and *play*... Abundance is a warm... *loving*... home... Abundance is having good friends... and *being* a good friend... Abundance is *giving*... and *receiving*... Abundance is *Love*...

See, sense and feel... abundance... *flowing*... in and around you...Welcome abundance...with *joy*... and *delight*...

Say to yourself... I now accept abundance into my life... I am a magnet for *all* good things... in the form of money... health... *loving* relationships... and *happiness*...

I am truly *thankful*... for *everything*... I have... in my life... *NOW*... I am ready... to manifest... my *best* life... and my Divine *purpose*... and I am *worthy*... of love... and all good things... *including* money...

I am now experiencing a *spiritual* expansion... of Divine love... in *every* area of my life... in my *work*... in my r*elationships*... in my *health*... and in my *finances*... I am ready to manifest... my dreams... in the form... of *prosperity*... loving *kindness*... and *abundance*...

I *know*... that *all* of my experiences... are stepping stones... on my path... to *love*... and I am *grateful*... for my life journey... I now go *forward*... on my *highest* path... with *love*... *joy*... and *abundance*... blessing *every* step of the way...

New *insights*... new *directions* ... are forming deep within me *now*... for me to use... later on... or right *now*... discovering new *abilities*... to rely on *myself*... to allow my *subconscious*... to give me the *right* information... at the right *time*... creating *perfect* opportunities... in an *easy* and *relaxed* manner... in *healthy* and *positive* ways... in *perfect* timing for *my* highest good... and the highest good of *all*... knowing that *positive* transformation... continues ... within you... at all times...

Note: If you plan to awaken after listening to this tape, use this ending:

As numbers are counted... from one to three... gently bring your awareness back to the current time and place... feeling refreshed and relaxed and energized... feeling wonderful and *opening your eyes* at the count of *three*...

One... you can take a nice deep breath... *Two*, coming up, coming *all the way up*... feeling very good, *much* better than before... and *Three*... *Three*... *opening your eyes*... Alert, Awake and Aware.

Note: If you plan to listen to this tape only when you're going to sleep, you might want to use the following ending instead:

If you are listening to this tape at night... or any time it is appropriate for you to fall asleep... you can fall asleep... anywhere along the way... and whenever you fall asleep... before you do... you can decide when... you want to wake up again... and even as you are sleeping and dreaming... *wonderful* dreams... your subconscious mind is *listening*... *learning*... *changing*... so you can... and *will*... accomplish your goals... *easily*... *effortlessly*... *permanently*...

And now... if it is your bedtime... you will continue sleeping... *deeply*... and *peacefully*... until you wake up tomorrow... feeling deeply *rested*... *energized*... and *inspired*... You wake up feeling *glad*... that you are *already* on your way...

Editor's Note: If you find you're not getting the desired results from this self-hypnosis script, consider seeking advice from a certified hypnotherapist.

Bibliography

Allen, Marc, *Visionary Business, An Entrepreneur's Guide to Success*. Novato, California: New World Library, 1995.

Allen, Marc, *The Millionaire Course*. Novato, California: New World Library, 2003.

Carroll, Leandra J., *The Architecture of All Abundance*. Novato, California: New World Library, 2001.

Dyer, Wayne, *The Power of Intention*. Carlsbad, California: Hay House, 2004.

Eker, T. Harv, *Secrets of the Millionaire Mind: Mastering the Inner Game of Wealth*. New York: Harper Business, 2005.

Gawain, Shakti, *Creative Visualization*. San Raphael, California: New World Library, 2002.

Hansen, Mark Victor and Robert G. Allen, *The One Minute Millionaire, The Enlightened Way to Wealth*. New York: Harmony Books, 2002.

Roberts, Jane, *The Nature of Personal Reality: (A Seth Book)* San Raphael, California: Amber-Allen Publishing, 1994.

Roman, Sanaya and Duane Packer, *Creating Money*. Tiburon, California: H.J. Kramer, 1988.

Stanley, Thomas J., *The Millionaire Mind*. Kansas City, Missouri: Andrews McMeel, 2000.

Luke Chao completed his Honors B.A. at the University of Toronto with a focus in English. A member of the National Guild of Hypnotists, he also helped to write *The Inner Power Series: Intuitive Security for Women*.

Linda Gabriel holds a BA and MFA from UCLA. A Certified Clinical Hypnotherapist, Linda specializes in helping people transform their lives by changing their minds. She presents clear and easy ways to dissolve the hidden inner stumbling blocks to abundance. A gifted teacher, Linda leads workshops throughout North America and maintains a private practice in Hollywood, California. She may be contacted through her website: www.lindagabriel.com